# TRUE
# TUSCAN

# TRUE TUSCAN

*Flavors and Memories*

*from the Countryside of Italy*

# CESARE CASELLA

HarperCollins*Publishers*

HarperCollins books may be purchased for educational, business, or sales promotional use.
For information, please write: Special Markets Department, HarperCollins Publishers,
10 East 53rd Street, New York, NY 10022.

FIRST EDITION

Designed by Joel Avirom and Jason Snyder

Printed on acid-free paper

Library of Congress Cataloging-in-Publication Data

Casella, Cesare.
True Tuscan / Casare Casella. — 1st ed.
p. cm.
Includes bibliographical references and index.
ISBN-10: 0-06-055555-6          ISBN-13: 978-0-06-055555-9
1. Cookery, Italian — Tuscan style. I. Title.

TX723.2.T86C3724 2005
641.5945'5 — dc22                    2004060550

05 06 07 08 09 ❖/RRD 10 9 8 7 6 5 4 3 2 1

*This book is dedicated to Chen,*
*my Tuscan in training.*

# ACKNOWLEDGMENTS

There are a handful of people who made this book possible, starting with my agent, David Black, who helped shepherd the manuscript from start to finish and provided advice and handholding at critical moments. Susan Friedland, my no-nonsense editor, has an unerring eye and a real love for Tuscan food; her guidance was invaluable. My editor Daniel Halpern was another great cheerleader who saw *True Tuscan* through to the end. My kitchen staff at Beppe, lead by Marc Taxiera, and with help from Daniele Gritzer, pitched in uncomplainingly for a year to test and retest and retest recipes until we got things right. Carlos Zuaghi and David Richter, John, Tom, and Theresa, were also part of the *True Tuscan* team. I'd like to thank the production, marketing, publicity, design, and copyediting people at HarperCollins, most of whom I never even met, but who created this book I love. I also owe a huge debt to Italian housewives who have been cooking the dishes in these pages for a thousand years, and who inspire me every day. Finally, there's my wife, Eileen Daspin. She worked, often at 4 A.M., to pull everything together, and now knows more about Apicius, ancient Roman cooking and Etruscan eating habits than she ever thought possible. *Mille grazie a tutti.*

# CONTENTS

# INTRODUCTION

◆

Children are rarely aware of the world outside their own. What they see and experience is what they think is normal for everyone. As far as I knew growing up, everyone everywhere who played ball ended up chasing it down into a field of wild fennel. Bonfires of rosemary, their scent filling the countryside, were burning in every town in the world. And all little boys spent their Octobers and Novembers getting up at the crack of dawn to help harvest the new crops of olives and grapes.

Now, of course, I know how special my childhood was and why the word *Tuscany* is so evocative for people—conjuring up the silver of olive trees, family trattorias, centuries-old farmhouses, and rolling hills as far as the eye can see. It's no wonder that marketers use the adjective *Tuscan* to promote kitchen design, olive oil, even classical music.

As Tuscany has been adopted by popular culture, I've started feeling evangelical. I want people to know *my* Tuscany, the place I grew up, the foods I ate, the world I consider True Tuscan. Don't get me wrong. I'm not a purist. I don't think everything has to be done the same way it was one hundred or two hundred years ago, with specific ingredients and presentation. If anything, it's the opposite. I love taking traditional dishes from Veneto, Puglia, even ancient Rome and translating them into something new. Cooking a dish like Pasta Norma (page 91), a Sicilian specialty, and putting my spin on it makes it Tuscan for me, because I'm Tuscan. That's what I mean by True Tuscan. It's cooking from both the heart and intellect, being flexible, curious, and generous. It's about one true Tuscan's approach to the kitchen—mine.

Consider my Pollo Fritto, fried chicken, on page 150. Not Tuscan? Well, it's my mom, Rosa's, recipe, a dish I ate my whole life before I moved to New York. She rubs the parts with lemon juice, dredges them in flour, dips them in beaten egg, then fries them all up to a crunchy gold. Believe it or not, she also throws some green tomatoes into the frying pan. My twist? A fat bouquet of fried rosemary, sage, and thyme sprigs with every order. What a mouthful: the salty, crisp crust, the crumbly herb leaves, and the juiciest chicken this side of the Arno.

Then there's the Maremmana, or ribs Tuscan cowboy style (page 172). I've taken no end of grief for them since the day we opened Beppe, my restaurant in New York. *Ribs? From Tuscany?* One outraged reviewer wanted to know how I could be serving cowboy-style ribs when there's no such thing as Tuscan cowboys. It was as if I had claimed peanut butter and jelly was invented in Lucca. For the record, the Maremma, a beautiful, hilly stretch of Tuscan coastline, is full not only of horses, cattle, ranches, and Italian cowboys, but also Italian cowboys who eat spareribs.

I make my spareribs *alla cacciatora*, or hunter's style, a tomato-olive preparation in Italy we usually only make for chicken or rabbit. It's called that because hunters used to pick olives when they were out in the countryside and bring them home for their wives who would roast them in the oven with salt to cut the bitterness and serve them along with the catch of the day. My spareribs are all about that sauce. Garlicky and spiked with rosemary, they taste like a night around a campfire. In what I like to think is typical Casella-style cooking, my spareribs take tradition (the sauce), marry it to the unconventional (the ribs) and finish with something new (sautéed broccoli rabe, a vegetable that is almost nonexistent in Tuscany as an accompaniment).

This style is what I call "free range," like the chicken that gets to roam, scratching for food everywhere. I take inspiration from all periods and all of Italy: There are ideas from my mom, others from my grandmother. There are twists I have swiped from my best friend in Viareggio, from Pontormo, from a Renaissance painter from Florence, and from Giacomo Puccini, the composer. And that's what makes my cooking authentic: Like the best Tuscan food, it's about invention.

Where I learned to cook, the most traditional recipes come from peasants and housewives, who used what they had on hand. Usually that meant a lot of beans (how else would Tuscans have been assigned the nickname *mangiafagioli*, or the bean-eaters?), cheap cuts of meat, and bread to stretch everything from soup to casseroles. We actually have a dish called *acquacotta*, or "cooked water" (page 62) that becomes a soup when a couple of vegetables and some herbs are thrown in for flavor, and that differs from town to town, too.

Luckily, I have more to work with than water and a few carrots, so *True Tuscan* is about that same resourceful and creative spirit. After spending thirty-five years in Tuscany, there's hardly a nook I don't know or a cranny I personally haven't visited, and *True* introduces readers to every bit of it. More than just a cookbook, it covers culture and history, from facts about the Etruscans to gossip about Catherine de' Medici, who introduced the French to the fork (not to mention high heels and women's underpants).

The book is organized the way Italians eat their meals, starting with *antipasti* (appetizers) followed by *primi* (first courses), *secondi* (second courses), *contorni* (side dishes), and *dolci* (desserts). Serving all these courses for Americans might seem overwhelming, but the key is portion size. Italians simply eat smaller portions than Americans do, so that a typical meal is five courses, including dessert. This number of courses is at least partially rooted in economics: By including pasta or soup in every meal, there was less need for meat, which until after World War II was too expensive for most Italians to serve. The practice persisted into good times though, and even today Italians still like their plate of pasta first.

You'll notice that with almost all dishes I suggest a wine, but I came close to not including wine recommendations. What made me hesitate was the mania that has taken over anything to do with wine lately, turning wine collecting and drinking into a competitive sport. But I love wine so much, especially Italian wine, and drinking it is such a big part of enjoying food, that it seemed silly not to. I'd like to encourage you to take a more relaxed, curious approach to wine, trying new ones rather than seeking out pricey known ones. All of the wines I suggest are Tuscan, because I know them best and because this is a book about Tuscan food. But they have counterparts from all over the world. Try them. If you can't find a specific wine, look for the grape or acidity I describe. You'll get to know wines much better that way.

In a nutshell: I feel it's better to pair wine with food of the same region. But basically you should drink what you like, whether it's the perfect theoretical pairing or not. While wine can certainly enhance the flavor of food, if you like Pinot Grigio (classically a fish or poultry wine) but you also like steak, enjoy them together. If you want Vin Santo with pork, so be it. I chill my red wine in summer and drink Champagne with ice cubes in it. That scandalizes some people, but it's how I like it. To me, it's all about taste and informing my palate.

The same philosophy applies throughout *True Tuscan*. This is a cookbook for Italophile food lovers and armchair chefs who want to eat and learn. It's not just about knowing how to make liver *crostini*, but why we eat *crostini* in Tuscany, how the specific recipe in Pistoia is different from the one in Montalcino, and who invented the concept in the first place. This is not a history book, but my take on culinary history and a guide for anyone who wants to know what it is like to be truly Tuscan.

# ABOUT THE RECIPES

As I say throughout, "True Tuscan," the quality that best defines a Tuscan chef, is flexibility. So, if I call for large shrimp in a recipe and all you can find are small, try it and see how it comes out—just keep an eye on the cooking times to adjust for the change. And if you can't find shrimp at all for the fish stew, add in some more firm white-fleshed fish. The same guideline goes for spices, cheeses, and meats. I believe in improvising.

On a similar but slightly different note, there are a few ingredients that I tend to refer to generically—eggs, for example. To me eggs imply large, but if you can only get small, adjust by adding an extra one to the recipe. Flour to me is all-purpose flour, but you can experiment with other types if you like. Also, milk should be whole unless you have a personal reason not to use it; substitute as necessary. I prefer sweet butter, but if you only have salted, use less salt in the rest of the recipe.

Lastly, I am a bit of a stickler for freshness, so if I say a teaspoon of lemon juice, I mean fresh-squeezed first, but if it's not available, I'd try fresh-squeezed lime juice, or depending on the recipe some other citrus or even a tiny splash of vinegar. I wouldn't *not* do a recipe because you can only find bottled lemon juice; you also might consider leaving it out.

# TRUE
# TUSCAN

# ANTIPASTI
## *Appetizers*

Over the years I've read various "theories" on antipasti, mostly having to do with foods designed to stimulate the appetite or somehow prepare the diner for the meal that follows. My own theory is that it's all about social order, that appetizers are a way of showing how refined a diner or his host is. Just look at Roman banquets. The Romans started their meals with eleven *ordover*, a Venetian word, which could include seasoned eggs, vegetables, cheeses, olives, and even fricassees that today would be complete meals in themselves. It was a way of showing off social position. I'm no blueblood, but I am a true believer in multiple courses. The trick, of course, is to serve food well, without overwhelming yourself with too much work or your guests with too much food.

In Tuscany, luckily, our appetizers are comparatively simple, the quintessential example being the *crostini*, or small pieces of toast spread with chicken liver pâté or other toppings. As far as I can tell, serving bread with a topping is a tradition with roots or at least a reference to the Middle Ages, when people tended to use thick slabs of bread to hold their food. Once plates became popular, the habit of bread with food remained (it's also an inexpensive way to stretch a dish). My guess is that over time the meal-sized bread with topping simply gave way to *crostini* proportions.

There are hundreds of variations on this theme, of course, and you can top *crostini* with everything from chick-peas in vinaigrette to leftover seafood salad, which is one of the aspects that makes Tuscan antipasti so easy to make. Back around the turn of the nineteenth century, anchovy and caviar *crostini* were popular and so were toast points topped with *musciame*, or salted dolphin meat. While eating dolphin is now illegal, I don't know why those others fell out of favor. If it were up to me, I'd put dozens of such forgotten dishes back in circulation. In fact, one of my "new" antipasti is actually about two thousand years old—oysters Apicius—a recipe I've updated (see page 20) from a Roman food lover who wrote what's considered the world's first cookbook, *De re coquinaria*, or *On Cooking*.

The other super-easy Tuscan antipasto is cold cuts, or *salumi* in Italian. The challenge is locating a reliable supplier who can track down the right varieties, from *finocchiona* (a salami studded with fennel seeds) to *salame toscano* (with whole peppercorns) to *bilordo*, a sausage made from organ meats and blood stuffed into the lining of a pig's stomach. Round those out with some prosciutto, breadsticks, and chunks of pecorino (sheep's milk) cheese and you have the most authentic Tuscan antipasto course there is. When selecting your own ingredients for antipasto, be flexible. I cheat with some nontraditional tidbits Americans love, like little squares of eggplant Parmesan, bean salad, and seafood salad. It's true to the spirit I espouse of adaptability and satisfies American tastes. Everyone ends up happier.

## FEGATELLI *alla* TOSCANA
### *Pork Liver Bundles with Fennel*

This is an Etruscan dish we eat today in the late fall after we've slaughtered the pigs and put the meat up for the winter. Traditionally it was prepared by alternating pieces of Tuscan bread with pork livers on skewers of bay leaf branches or wild fennel stalks. After they were cooked, we'd take the livers off the skewers and eat them hot. I've updated the recipe, roasting the liver in a casserole without the bread but with a mixture of bread crumbs, pancetta, fennel seeds, and crumbled bay leaves. The tricky part may be finding both the pork liver and the caul, or "lace fat," which comes from the pig's stomach and looks like a lacy net. (It's used to wrap pâtés and melts during the cooking process.) If your butcher doesn't carry it, use thin slices of pancetta to secure the bundles. Calf's liver is an acceptable, though not ideal, substitute for the pork liver.

**SERVES 4**

**WINE SUGGESTION:** *Something with nice acidity, like a Sauvignon Blanc or Vermentino, goes great with the liver here. I like Michele Satta's Costa di Giulia, which is a blend of both types of grapes.*

½ cup Bread Crumbs (page 27)

2 tablespoons grated Parmesan cheese

2 teaspoons finely chopped bay leaves, plus 8 whole ones

1½ tablespoons finely chopped fresh sage

1 teaspoon ground fennel seed

4 ounces finely chopped pancetta (1 cup)

Salt

Freshly ground black pepper

1 pound pork liver, cut into 1-inch squares (must be special-ordered from a butcher; or you can substitute calf's liver)

½ pound caul fat, cut into 3-inch pieces (or thin slices of pancetta)

2 tablespoons extra virgin olive oil

1 Preheat the oven to 400° F.

2 In a bowl combine the bread crumbs, Parmesan, chopped bay leaves, sage, fennel seed, pancetta, and salt and pepper to taste.

3 Add the liver squares and toss in the crumb mixture to coat completely.

4 Wrap each liver square in a piece of the caul fat to form a bundle (or use thin slices of pancetta) and secure with toothpicks.

5 Coat an ovenproof casserole with the olive oil and arrange the "bundles" in an even single layer in it. Place the remaining whole bay leaves in between the bundles.

6 Roast for 30 to 40 minutes, or until the liver is cooked through and the caul fat starts to look golden. Serve immediately.

# CIBREO

## Catherine's Chicken Livers

I have a cousin, Elsa, who likes chicken livers so much, she eats them raw. This is pretty extreme even for a country kid like me, but it doesn't beat Catherine de' Medici, who ate so many chicken livers on her thirtieth birthday that she almost died of indigestion. I think the queen's staff used a recipe different from mine, since in Catherine's era, *cibreo* was made with cockscomb and wattle, which are pretty hard to get these days. I serve this over toast.

SERVES 4

Flour for dredging

Pinch ground cinnamon

Pinch grated nutmeg

Salt

Freshly ground black pepper

1 pound chicken livers, trimmed of fat

3 tablespoons extra virgin olive oil

½ cup finely chopped onion

1 teaspoon minced garlic, plus 1 whole clove

2 tablespoons chopped anchovy fillets (about 6) in oil. (I prefer the taste of salted anchovies, but they need to be soaked in white wine or water for a few hours or overnight before using.)

2 tablespoons capers in brine, rinsed (I prefer capers packed in salt because they have more flavor, but you need to rinse and soak them in water for at least 6 hours before using.)

2 tablespoons finely chopped fresh sage

½ cup dry marsala or sweet vermouth

1½ cups chicken stock

2 egg yolks

1 teaspoon lemon juice

4 slices Tuscan bread

WINE SUGGESTION: *I'd go with a Tuscan Chardonnay or Vernaccia, a medium-bodied white from the town of San Gimignano. Castello di Montauto has a good Vernaccia that makes me think of apples.*

1  In a large bowl combine the flour, cinnamon, nutmeg, and salt and pepper to taste. Add the chicken livers and coat them with the flour mixture. Shake off any excess.

2  Heat the oil in a large skillet over medium heat. Add the chicken livers and brown on both sides.

3  Add the onion, garlic, anchovies, capers, and sage and continue cooking until the onion is translucent, 7 to 8 minutes.

4  Add the marsala and cook until it has reduced by half.

5  Add the chicken stock and simmer still over medium heat for 10 minutes. Meanwhile, in a bowl beat the egg yolks with the lemon juice until smooth.

6  Toast or grill the bread and rub each slice with the remaining garlic clove. Set aside.

7  Slowly stir the yolk mixture into the pan with the chicken livers. Make sure the egg yolks don't scramble. When done, the sauce should be a velvety consistency that coats the livers. Taste for seasonings and serve on the toasted bread slices.

### • CATHERINE DE' MEDICI •

There are plenty of reasons Catherine de' Medici couldn't win a popularity contest: When she was queen of France, she lured thousands of French Protestants to Paris for a big wedding and then had them all killed; she also liked poisoning her enemies and helped start a number of wars.

On the plus side, when Catherine moved from Florence to Paris, she introduced France to everything from artichokes to forks. Culinary historians disagree, but there's evidence some of the food we now think of as French actually came from Tuscany. The queen, who at just under five feet, had the first high heels made for her wedding, also brought with her melons, peas, truffles, macaroons, guinea hen, zabaglione, and frangipane tarts. One of my all-time favorite dishes is thought to be a Catherine de' Medici export to France: orange duck, made with fruit from a famous Florentine garden.

As I see it, Catherine helped modernize France foodwise. The future queen turned her French chefs on to sauces and thankfully got the French court to separate sweet and savory dishes. But the piece of Catherine culinary trivia I like best has to do with her Tuscan cousin, Maria de' Medici, who also married a French royal. Like her cousin, Maria brought some Italian cooking techniques to France. One immediate hit was puff pastry. In my book, that means we Tuscans had a hand in the birth of the croissant.

# INVOLTINI *di* CAVOLO
## *Stuffed Cabbage*

Stuffed cabbage was the way my grandmother used inexpensive pieces of meat she had in the kitchen, and I always thought it was so clever of her to come up with the dish. Then I came to New York and every other Jewish deli had a version of stuffed cabbage. For the life of me, I couldn't figure out how the Jews had discovered my grandmother's idea! Now I know there's no connection—my grandmother's version has cheese and pork in it, which is about as unkosher as you can get—but I still laugh over my initial reaction. **SERVES 4**

**THE STUFFING**

1 cup day-old Tuscan bread, crusts removed, cut into cubes

¼ cup milk

½ pound ground pork

⅓ cup chopped onion

2 teaspoons minced garlic

2 tablespoons finely chopped fresh Italian parsley

1 egg

2 tablespoons grated Parmesan cheese, plus a little more for finishing

1 pinch each of ground cinnamon, nutmeg, cloves, coriander, and ginger

Salt

Fresh ground black pepper

**THE CABBAGE**

2 tablespoons red wine vinegar

1 large head savoy cabbage, leaves separated and tough ribs removed

3 tablespoons extra virgin olive oil

3 cups sliced carrots

⅔ cup chopped onion

2 teaspoons chopped garlic

4 cups sliced celery

½ cup dry white wine

½ cup canned whole tomatoes with their juice, pureed (You can also use canned, pureed tomatoes, but I think whole ones are less acidic and of better quality.)

1½ cups chicken stock

1 teaspoon fresh thyme leaves

Flour for dusting

2 tablespoons lemon juice

1 Make the stuffing: Let the bread soak in the milk for 15 to 20 minutes, or until all the bread is soft. Squeeze out any excess milk.

2 In a large bowl combine the pork, ⅓ cup of the onion, the garlic, parsley, egg, the 2 tablespoons Parmesan, and the spices. Season with salt and pepper to taste. Make sure the mixture is well combined, then set aside.

WINE SUGGESTION: *Frescobaldi Pomino Rosso is a perfect match here because it's so soft and velvety. It's made mostly with Pinot Nero and Sangiovese grapes, but you can also look for something that's all Pinot Nero.*

3 Prepare the cabbage: Bring a large pot of salted water to a boil with red wine vinegar. Prepare a large bowl of ice water. Cook the cabbage in the vinegar water for 2 to 3 minutes. Remove the cabbage from the water, drain, and plunge into the bowl of ice water. Remove and pat dry.

4 Lay the cabbage leaves out on a flat surface. Place 3 to 4 tablespoons of the stuffing in the center of each cabbage leaf. Roll the cabbage leaf around the stuffing tucking in each end. Place the leaves seam side down so that they do not unroll.

5 Coat the bottom of a large skillet with the olive oil and add the carrots, onion, celery, and garlic. Sauté over medium heat until the onion becomes translucent, 7 to 8 minutes.

6 Add the wine and reduce by half.

7 Add the pureed tomatoes, chicken stock, thyme, and season with salt and pepper.

8 Dust the cabbage rolls lightly with flour and add them to the pan. Cover and simmer for 10 minutes. Stir in the lemon juice and adjust the seasonings.

9 Place a few cabbage rolls on each plate and spoon some broth and vegetables on top. Sprinkle lightly with grated Parmesan before serving.

# SALSICCIA
## *Homemade Sausage*

The idea of using scrap meats for sausage, preserving them with salts and using spices and herbs as flavoring agents, has been around at least since Roman times, and every region in Italy has its own distinctive mix of flavors and meats. In Tuscany we primarily stick to fresh pork sausage, which I like to spice up with *spezie forti*—a potent spice mix of black pepper, cloves, nutmeg, and a hint of cinnamon. (I have my own version, called Tuscan Spice, which I make and sell through my company, Republic of Beans. See Sources on page 221.) Be sure to rinse and soak the sausage casings 24 hours before using them. Grill the sausages, then serve them over cannellini beans and they are pretty hard to beat.

SERVES 10 TO 12, ABOUT 25 SAUSAGES

5 pounds ground pork butt, shoulder, or other cuts

2 tablespoons freshly ground black pepper

2 tablespoons Tuscan Spice (see headnote) (Or use *garam masala*, or mix together equal parts of ground allspice, cinnamon, nutmeg, and cloves.)

1½ teaspoons chopped garlic, marinated in a glass of red wine for 1 hour

½ tablespoon fennel pollen or ground fennel seeds (fennel pollen is an intense anise-flavored powder)

⅓ cup kosher salt

½ pound sausage casings (Ask your butcher or see Sources on page 221; the casings must be rinsed and soaked for 24 hours before using.)

5–6 cups cooked cannellini beans (page 187)

___

WINE SUGGESTION: *Any simple Rosso di Montalcino would go great with these sausages. One I'm partial to is made by Casanova di Neri; and in the summertime, I drink it slightly chilled.*

___

1  Mix all of the ingredients (except the casings and beans) in a large bowl until the spices are well incorporated.

**2** Using the sausage attachment of your mixer or a sausage machine, fill casings with the forcemeat, creating links that are 5 inches long. Twist 4 or 5 times between links, tying off each end with a piece of fine kitchen twine. If you don't have casing, shape the pork mixture into meatballs or 5-inch torpedoes.

**3** Place the sausages in the refrigerator for 2 hours, then grill. Or store the sausages in the refrigerator for up to 2 days before grilling.

**4** Before grilling, prick the sausages all over with a skewer or use a sharp knife to slice a lengthwise slit in the casing. This will allow steam to escape while cooking. Grill sausages for 5 to 10 minutes, turning, until they are cooked through. The juices should run clear when done. Serve the sausages hot off the grill with cooked cannellini beans.

# PATATE *e* CARCIOFI
## *Potato and Artichoke Tart*

I like artichokes because they are so versatile. There are the baby ones sliced thin and tossed with Parmesan and olive oil with a touch of marjoram, and the Roman ones, which are fried whole. Back in the 1960s, Italy's favorite way to serve artichokes was as a digestive, in a drink called Cinar. I still remember the Cinar ad: A man was sitting in a chair in the middle of a traffic jam, calmly sipping his Cinar, and the tagline was, "Drink Cinar to beat the stress of modern life."

This is a recipe my aunt used to make. It was a way to make just a few artichokes go a long way since the potatoes soak up the artichoke flavor. I like it as a side dish. **SERVES 6**

1 pound potatoes, peeled and cut into 1-inch dice (3 cups)

Salt

1 medium lemon

6 baby artichokes or 2 globe artichoke bottoms

5 tablespoons extra virgin olive oil

1 tablespoon chopped garlic

1 teaspoon finely chopped fresh thyme

¼ cup dry white wine

2 eggs, beaten

2 tablespoons butter

2 tablespoons finely chopped fresh Italian parsley

Freshly ground black pepper

---

**WINE SUGGESTION:** *Artichokes can be a hard match with wine, but a good varietal to look for is Ansonica, which dates back to Etruscan times. There's also a wine I like called Ansonica made by Parrina.*

---

1 Put the diced potatoes in a saucepan, cover with cold water, and season generously with salt. Bring to a boil and cook until the potatoes are very tender and almost falling apart, about 20 to 25 minutes. Test after 15 minutes in case they are ready earlier. Drain and reserve in a bowl.

2 Fill a bowl with water. Cut the lemon in half, squeeze the juice into the water, and add the squeezed lemon halves, too. Peel the outer leaves from the artichokes until you reach the part where the leaves are mostly a creamy yellow. Cut the top inch off each artichoke and trim away the stem so that you are left with a golf-ball-sized heart. Slice the hearts thin and add to the lemon water. (For globe artichokes, remove the tough outer leaves and cut the artichokes into wedges. Remove the choke and the soft curly leaves above it. Slice thin and place in the lemon water.) Set aside.

3 Lightly mash the boiled potatoes.

4 Place 2½ tablespoons of the olive oil, the garlic, and thyme in a large sauté pan and sauté over medium until the garlic is golden, 3 to 5 minutes.

5 Drain the artichokes, add them to the pan, and season with salt and pepper. Cook for 5 minutes. Add the wine and cook until it has reduced by half.

6 Add 1 cup of water to the pan and cook the artichokes until the leaves have fallen off the hearts, and the hearts are soft. Remove from the heat.

7 Mix the eggs, butter, parsley, and salt and pepper to taste into the mashed potatoes. Add the artichokes and stir to combine well.

8 Heat the remaining 2½ tablespoons olive oil in a large nonstick frying pan over medium heat. Add the potato mixture to the pan and press it down to form a thick pancake. Fry the pancake until it is crispy about 4 to 5 minutes; flip and cook the other side another 4 to 5 minutes. Remove, slice into wedges, and serve either hot or at room temperature.

# PORREA

## *Leek Tart*

Spend enough time in Tuscan restaurants and you can't help but notice all the variations on savory pies. There's *ciancifricola*, *erbolata*, and *porrata*—all tarts made with vegetables and eggs, but with different vegetables as highlights. This recipe is for *porrea*, a leek and sausage combination that the monks of San Lorenzo in Florence served in the 1300s to celebrate an important religious holiday. These days we eat it just because we like it. **SERVES 6**

### THE CRUST

4 cups flour

2 tablespoons sugar

2 teaspoons salt

1 teaspoon freshly ground black pepper

½ pound (1 cup) cold butter, cut into pea-sized pieces

4 eggs

### THE FILLING

¼ cup extra virgin olive oil

2 teaspoons minced garlic

½ cup finely chopped onion

Pinch crushed red pepper

¾ pound fresh sausage (half sweet and half hot), removed from casing and crumbled

¼ pound (1 cup) minced prosciutto

4 cups coarsely chopped leeks (white and green parts)

½ cup dry white wine

2 eggs

3 tablespoons grated Parmesan cheese

Pinch grated nutmeg

Salt

Freshly ground black pepper

Eggwash: 1 egg beaten with 1 tablespoon water

---

**WINE SUGGESTION:** *A Chianti Classico is nice here, and for something special, you could try a Chianti Rufina like Castello di Nipozzano Riserva, which is plumy and fresh.*

---

1　Make the crust: In a food processor combine the flour, sugar, salt, and pepper. Add the butter and pulse until the mixture looks like cornmeal. Add the eggs and pulse another two or three times. Add 1 to 2 tablespoons water if the mixture is very dry. Turn the contents of the bowl out onto a clean work surface and gather the dough together with your hands. Form into a disk, wrap in plastic, and refrigerate for at least 30 minutes or at most 24 hours.

2　Preheat the oven to 375° F.

3　Make the filling: Cover the bottom of a large skillet with the olive oil. Add the garlic, onion, and crushed red pepper and sauté over medium until the onion is translucent and very aromatic, about 10 minutes. Add the sausage, prosciutto, leeks, and wine and simmer for 25 minutes, until the mixture has reduced almost completely and the mixture is not too wet. Remove the pan from the heat and let cool.

4　Stir the eggs, Parmesan, nutmeg, and salt and pepper to taste into the sausage mixture.

5　Butter and flour a 10-inch pie plate. Remove the dough from the refrigerator and cut it into 2 unequal parts, about a one third to two thirds split. On a floured surface roll the larger piece of dough into a circle about ⅛ inch thick, with a 15-inch diameter. Place the dough in the prepared pie plate. There should be a large overhang.

6　Spoon the filling into the lined pie plate.

7　On the floured surface roll the remaining dough into a circle ⅛ inch thick, with a 12-inch diameter. Place the dough over the filling.

8　Using kitchen shears or a sharp knife, trim the top crust so it just meets the sides of the pie plate. Brush with the egg wash. Fold the overhanging dough up over the top crust and brush with the egg wash. Cut several holes in the top crust to allow steam to escape.

9　Bake the tart 45 to 50 minutes, until the crust is light brown, smooth, and shiny. Let the tart stand for at least 20 minutes before serving. Serve hot or at room temperature.

# TORTA D'ERBE

## *Springtime Vegetable Pie*

Way before the Medicis snacked on this pie, it was a favorite with the Romans. It can be simplified by using just Swiss chard, eggs, and cheese, but I like all the extra ingredients, especially the sausage. This is more of an appetizer or afternoon snack in Italy, but I'd serve it here to friends at home for brunch any day. You can also make a well in the filling and break a whole egg into it before adding the top crust. **SERVES 6 TO 8**

### THE CRUST

4 cups flour

2 tablespoons sugar

2 teaspoons salt

1 teaspoon freshly ground black pepper

16 tablespoons (2 sticks) cold butter, cut into pea-sized pieces

4 eggs

### THE FILLING

1½ cups ricotta cheese

3 tablespoons extra virgin olive oil

½ pound sweet Italian sausage, removed from casing and crumbled

2 tablespoons butter

1 pound (8 cups) Swiss chard, washed, stems cut into 1-inch lengths, and leaves chopped

1 pound asparagus, tough ends removed and cut into 1-inch lengths

2 cups peas, fresh or frozen

Salt

Freshly ground black pepper

½ teaspoon Tuscan Spice (see Sources on page 221) or use *garam masala*, or mix together equal parts of ground allspice, cinnamon, nutmeg, and cloves

¾ cup grated Parmesan cheese

3 eggs

2 teaspoons finely chopped fresh marjoram

Pinch grated nutmeg

Eggwash: 1 egg beaten with 1 tablespoon water

---

**WINE SUGGESTION:** *Because of all the vegetables here, you could go with either white or red. Morellino di Scansano from the producer Lohsa is a red I like a lot. It's from the up-and-coming wine area, Maremma.*

---

1 Make the crust: In a food processor combine the flour, sugar, salt and pepper. Add the butter and pulse until the mixture looks like cornmeal. Add the eggs and pulse another two or three times. Add 1 to 2 tablespoons water if the mixture is very dry. Turn the contents of the bowl out onto a clean work surface and gather the dough together with your hands. Form into a disk, wrap in plastic, and refrigerate for at least 30 minutes or at most 24 hours.

2 Make the filling: Place the ricotta in a mesh strainer to allow the excess water to drain off. Set aside. Prepare a large bowl of salted ice water.

3 Coat the bottom of a large skillet with the olive oil and heat over medium heat. Add the sausage and sauté until browned. Remove from the pan and reserve.

4 In another large skillet melt the butter. When the melted butter just starts to sizzle, add the Swiss chard and sauté for 5 to 6 minutes. Season with salt and pepper. When the Swiss chard is very soft, transfer it to a strainer or colander set over a dish and cool in the refrigerator. Once cooled, squeeze the chard with your hands to remove the excess water. It should be as dry as possible.

5 In a large bowl combine well the Tuscan spice, asparagus, sausage, Swiss chard, peas, ricotta, Parmesan, eggs, marjoram, nutmeg, and salt and pepper. Set aside.

6 Preheat the oven to 350° F. Butter and flour two 8-inch pie plates.

7 Remove the dough from the refrigerator and divide it into 4 pieces, 2 larger, 2 smaller. On a floured work surface roll out the larger pieces of dough until they are about ⅛ inch thick. Line the prepared pie plates with the rolled-out dough; the dough should be larger than the pie plate and hang over the edges. Roll out the smaller pieces of dough and reserve.

8 Divide the filling between the dough-lined pie plates. Place the smaller pieces of dough on top of the filling. Using kitchen scissors trim the top dough so that the edges come to the sides of the pie plate. Brush with the eggwash. Fold the overhanging edges of the bottom layer up over the top dough. Press to seal the crusts together and then brush the edges with the eggwash. Cut 3 or 4 holes in the top crust to allow steam to escape.

9 Bake the pies for 1 hour. When done the crust should be firm, shiny, and golden. Let the pies stand for at least 20 minutes but not more than an hour before serving.

# PAN LAVATO

## *Baked Cauliflower Renaissance Style*

I first learned about *pan lavato* (it means washed bread) when I read the fourteenth-century author Boccaccio. This is my version. **SERVES** 6

Salt

4 cups cauliflower florets

6 tablespoons extra virgin olive oil

2 tablespoons chopped anchovy fillets (about 6) in oil. (I prefer the taste of salted anchovies, but they need to be soaked in white wine or water for a few hours or overnight before using.)

6 whole garlic cloves, crushed

3 tablespoons red wine vinegar

Freshly ground black pepper

6 slices day-old Tuscan bread, cut ¼ inch thick and grilled (If you can't find Tuscan bread, any crusty loaf will do, but the bread must be completely dry and crisp, otherwise the dish will be mushy.)

4 tablespoons grated Parmesan cheese

---

**WINE SUGGESTION:** *A young Chianti is the best way to go with this dish. I like Chianti Spalletti from the area Pontassieve.*

---

1 Preheat the oven to 375° F.

2 Place 4 cups water in a medium saucepan, salt well, and bring to a boil. Add the cauliflower and cook for 15 minutes, or until tender. Remove the pan from the heat, leaving the cauliflower in the water.

3 Coat the bottom of a large skillet with 3 tablespoons of the olive oil. Add the anchovies and crushed garlic and sauté over medium heat until the garlic is golden. Add salt (sparingly, the anchovies are very salty) and fresh pepper to taste.

4 Remove the pan from the heat and stir in the vinegar.

5 Drain the cauliflower, reserving the cooking water, and place the cauliflower in a large bowl.

6 Add the anchovy mixture and 2 cups of the cooking water and combine very well.

7 Use the remaining 3 tablespoons of olive oil to grease a 12- by 10- by 2-inch ovenproof dish (4 quarts) that you can bring to the table. Cover the bottom with a layer of the bread and alternate with layers of the cauliflower mixture. Sprinkle the top with the Parmesan cheese.

8 Bake the dish for 20 minutes, or until the cheese is golden brown. Serve immediately.

# OCCHIO *di* BUE

## *Bull's Eye*

Florentines have eaten their asparagus boiled, tossed in butter, salt, and Parmesan cheese, then tucked under fried eggs for hundreds of years. I like to serve *occhio di bue* as a warm-up to dinner, but light eaters might prefer it instead of pasta or a meat course. **SERVES 4 TO 6**

Salt

2 pounds asparagus

2 tablespoons extra virgin olive oil

6 eggs

Freshly ground black pepper

¼ cup grated Parmesan cheese

1 teaspoon balsamic vinegar

¾ tablespoon grated lemon zest

**WINE SUGGESTION:** *To compliment the eggs, I'd try a Chardonnay, preferably a Tuscan one called Pomino Bianco Benefizio.*

1  Preheat the oven to 425° F.

2  Prepare a large bowl of salted ice water.

3  Bring a pot of well salted water to a boil. Snap the tough ends off the asparagus, add the asparagus to the pot, and blanch for 3 to 4 minutes. Remove to the bowl of salted ice water for 1 to 2 minutes, then drain. Slice each spear in half lengthwise and reserve.

4  Coat two 12-inch nonstick ovenproof pans with 1 tablespoon of the olive oil each. Place half of the spears in each pan. Crack 3 of the eggs over each pan of spears, season with salt and pepper, and place the pans in the oven. Cook for a few minutes until the whites of the eggs are set, then sprinkle each pan with 2 tablespoons of the grated Parmesan.

5  Return the pans to the oven for another 1 to 2 minutes, until the cheese has melted. When ready, the whites should be set but the yolks still runny.

6  Drizzle the spears with the balsamic vinegar, sprinkle with the grated lemon zest, and serve immediately.

# OSTRICHE *alla* FIORENTINA

## *Oysters Florentine*

Spinach isn't a signature ingredient of Florentine cooking or even as popular there as Swiss chard is, but many people still refer to dishes served on a bed of spinach as *à la Florentine*, or in the style of Florence. That is largely due to Catherine de' Medici, a Florentine who became the queen of France. She popularized spinach with her subjects and the association just stuck. Americans have a similar dish, oysters Rockefeller, named after John D. Rockefeller—either because the dish was so rich or because the spinach was the same color as money. **SERVES 4**

1½ pounds fresh spinach, well washed

4 tablespoons extra virgin olive oil

2 tablespoons thinly sliced garlic

3 ounces finely chopped pancetta or bacon (¾ cup)

Salt

Freshly ground black pepper

1 cup Béchamel Sauce (page 86)

4 tablespoons grated Parmesan cheese

Pinch of Tuscan Spice (see Sources on page 221), *garam masala*, or mix together equal parts of ground allspice, cinnamon, nutmeg, and cloves

20 oysters, such as Wellfleet or Bluepoint

One 3-pound box rock salt

2 tablespoons dried Bread Crumbs (page 27)

---

**WINE SUGGESTION:** *A Chardonnay or Pinot Bianco would compliment both the sweet oysters and creamy sauce. Look for Batàr, a medium-bodied white from Tuscany—a blend of both grapes—by Querciabella.*

---

1  Preheat the oven to 450° F.

2  Place the spinach with water still clinging to the leaves in a large pot. Cover and cook over medium heat, stirring occasionally, until it just wilts. Drain the spinach well in a colander, pressing out all excess water with the back of a spoon. Let cool and chop. Set aside.

3  Combine the olive oil, garlic and pancetta in a large skillet and sauté over medium heat. When the pancetta has browned lightly, add the spinach and sauté for a few minutes. Season with salt and pepper.

4 In a large bowl combine the sautéed spinach mixture with the Béchamel, Parmesan, and Tuscan spice.

5 Shuck the oysters, reserving the liquid, and set the oysters aside. Scrub the bottom shells clean, then place the shells on a large baking sheet and bake for 20 minutes. Remove and reserve.

6 Line the baking sheet with rock salt.

7 Stir half the reserved oyster liquid into the spinach mixture. Place an oyster into each of the prepared shells. Top with a spoonful of the spinach mixture and sprinkle each with bread crumbs. Nestle the shells in the salt on the baking sheet.

8 Bake for 5 to 7 minutes, or until the bread crumbs are brown and crispy. Serve immediately.

# OSTRICHE APICIUS

## *Oysters Apicius*

Most people wouldn't make a connection between farmed oyster beds and showers, but they were actually invented by the same person, Sergius Orata, in the first century B.C. I'm grateful for both creations, but I'd bet your average Roman would have voted for oyster beds over showers: Romans were big oyster eaters and did them up with ingredients like cilantro, lovage, wine, and a touch of honey. If you don't like cilantro, add more parsley. **SERVES 4**

20 large oysters, such as Wellfleet, belon, or Bluepoint

4 garlic cloves

2 tablespoons finely chopped fresh cilantro

1 teaspoon ground cumin

1 tablespoon chopped anchovy fillets (about 3) in oil. (I prefer the taste of salted anchovies, but they need to be soaked in white wine or water for a few hours or overnight before using.)

1 tablespoon honey

1 tablespoon red wine vinegar

½ cup Bread Crumbs (page 27)

¼ cup grated Parmesan cheese

2 ounces pancetta or bacon, minced (½ cup)

2 tablespoons finely chopped fresh Italian parsley

¼ cup toasted, finely chopped walnuts

Salt

Freshly ground black pepper

One 3-pound box of rock salt

---

**WINE SUGGESTION:** *Champagne, especially a* rosé. *Or look for a non-oakey Chardonnay from Tuscany, such as Fontarca Chardonnay D'Alessandro.*

---

1  Preheat the oven to 450° F.

2  Shuck the oysters over a bowl to collect all of the liquor. Reserve the oysters in the liquor.

3  Scrub the oyster shells clean, place them on a large baking sheet, and bake for 20 minutes. Remove and reserve.

**4** In a food processor puree the garlic, cilantro, cumin, anchovies, honey, vinegar, bread crumbs, Parmesan, and parsley. Stir in the pancetta and the walnuts by hand and season with salt and pepper. Set aside.

**5** Line a baking pan with a thick layer of the rock salt. Nestle the oyster shells in the salt and place an oyster in each shell. Sprinkle with the topping mixture and bake until golden brown, about 5 minutes.

**6** Use tongs to serve the oysters because the shells will be very hot. Serve at once.

## • APICIUS •

Every few years, foodies stumble over a different historical figure and get all worked up about his or her invaluable contribution to food. The latest character to be "discovered" is the well-to-do Roman, Marcus Gavius Apicius, who wrote *De re coquinaria*, one of the first recorded cookbooks, and a great window on the diet of the first century.

Apicius not only came up with the idea for making *foie gras*, he also experimented with everything from flamingo to camel and spent most of his fortune just eating well, or at least trying to eat well. In one story I read, he hired a boat and crew and set sail for North Africa in search of some giant prawns he heard were particularly good. When it turned out the prawns were just run of the mill, he turned around and sailed back to Rome.

Having once driven two straight days for reservations at the restaurants of Fredy Giradet, Paul Bocuse, and Alain Chapel in France and Switzerland, I can identify with the impulse to take this kind of trip. But the endless culinary excursions eventually took their toll on Apicius's bank account. When he realized he'd spent almost all of his fortune, the great gourmand decided to take his own life rather than just scrape by.

# INSALATA *di* POLPO

## *Octopus Salad*

I like octopus the way they eat it in Pisa, mixed with cannellini beans, a dish the Pisans call a "bis" or perfect pair. In this version, you can also cook the octopus the day before, marinate it overnight, and assemble the salad before serving. While it is good cold, I like to reheat the salad before giving it to my guests. **SERVES 6**

2 pounds fresh baby octopus (Ask your fishmonger to clean them or see How to Clean an Octopus on page 23.)

1 carrot

1 onion

1 celery stalk

1 lemon, quartered, plus 2 tablespoons fresh lemon juice

6 black peppercorns

Salt

½ cup red wine vinegar

1 tablespoon minced garlic

7 tablespoons extra virgin olive oil

Freshly ground black pepper

2 cups cooked cannellini beans (page 187)

2 tablespoons finely chopped fresh Italian parsley

2 cups chopped arugula or radicchio, or a combination of both (optional)

---

**WINE SUGGESTION:** *A Tuscan Chardonnay or a medium-bodied white like Le Bruniche, which is so smooth that it reminds me of caramel, would be lovely here.*

---

1 Place the octopus in a large pot with 4 quarts of water, the carrot, onion, celery, lemon quarters, peppercorns, ½ cup salt, and ¼ cup of the vinegar. Bring to a boil, turn down the heat, and simmer for 50 to 60 minutes, or until tender. (If you can't find baby octopus and use regular octopus, it will need to cook 2 hours.) Remove from heat and let cool in the water.

2 Preheat the oven to 450° F.

**3** Place the octopus on a baking sheet and bake for about 5 minutes. Remove and cut into 1-inch pieces.

**4** In a bowl combine the remaining ¼ cup red wine vinegar, garlic, ¼ cup of the olive oil, and salt and pepper to taste. Add the octopus and marinate in the refrigerator for at least 1 hour or up to 24 hours.

**5** Combine the cooked beans, parsley, and remaining lemon juice in a bowl. Add the octopus and mix well. I suggest reheating briefly before serving, though it is also good cold. If using, add the arugula and radicchio now. Toss the salad with the remaining 3 tablespoons olive oil and season with salt and pepper to taste.

## • HOW TO CLEAN AN OCTOPUS •

If you're feeling ambitious and want to clean an octopus yourself, here's the fastest way to do it. Wear surgical gloves and be prepared for a mess. Clean out the belly (the big bulbous part above the eyes) and discard all the contents. Sprinkle the octopus with ¼ cup kosher salt and use your hands to scrub the octopus. Make sure to cover all parts of the octopus, including the suction cups on the tentacles. After thoroughly scrubbing the octopus, douse it with 1 cup red wine vinegar and massage it for another 2 to 3 minutes. Then rinse thoroughly with cold water.

# SOPPRESSATA di POLPO

## *Octopus Salami*

I first made this dish years ago after I had something similar at my friend Lorenzo's restaurant in Forte di Marmi. The octopus looks spectacular on a plate and is easy to make. It took me a few times to figure out how to compress the octopus into a salami, but I ended up just using a loaf pan and weighting it down with a brick. You will have leftover dressing, which will keep in a covered container in the refrigerator for up to two weeks. Use it on salads or warm it slightly and spoon it over white-fleshed fish. This is a definite do-ahead recipe. **SERVES 6 TO 8**

4 whole canned plum tomatoes drained, cut in half lengthwise, and seeds removed

Salt

1 cup pitted black Italian olives

1 tablespoon capers in brine, rinsed (I prefer capers packed in salt because they have more flavor, but you need to rinse and soak them in water for at least 6 hours before using.)

2⅓ cups red wine vinegar

¼ cup finely diced red onion

2 tablespoons finely chopped fresh Italian parsley, plus 2 sprigs

1 cup extra virgin olive oil

Freshly ground black pepper

1 cup thinly sliced red onions

1 celery stalk, roughly chopped

1 carrot, roughly chopped

2 red onions, roughly chopped

10 garlic cloves

2 sprigs fresh rosemary

2 sprigs fresh thyme

1 sprig fresh sage

1 tablespoon whole black peppercorns

One 2-pound octopus (ask your fishmonger to clean it or see How to Clean an Octopus on page 23.)

6 cups arugula

**WINE SUGGESTION:** *The seaside area called Maremma has become a leader in the last few years in interesting wines. I like the full-bodied white Vermentino, which comes from that region. One good one to look for is Litorale Vermentino.*

1 Preheat the oven to 250° F.

2 Spread the tomatoes on a baking sheet and sprinkle with salt. Bake until the tomatoes are very dry, about 45 minutes. Finely chop.

3 In a food processor puree the olives, capers, tomatoes, and ⅓ cup of the vinegar until smooth. Stir in the ¼ cup finely diced onion and the 2 tablespoons finely chopped parsley and puree. With the machine running, drizzle in the olive oil and ground pepper to taste. Adjust the seasonings and refrigerate. (This makes 2½ cups dressing, but you will only need about a third; use the leftover dressing for other salads. The dressing will keep for up to 2 weeks in the refrigerator.)

4 Put the 1 cup thinly sliced onions in a bowl with 1 cup of the remaining red wine vinegar. Set aside to marinate for 2 to 3 hours.

5 Using a 6-inch square of cheesecloth and string, make a large bundle containing the celery, carrot, chopped onions, garlic, and the sprigs of rosemary, thyme, sage, and parsley. Put the bundle in a 12-quart stock pot and add the remaining 1 cup vinegar, ½ cup salt, peppercorns, and octopus. Fill the pot with water, bring to a boil, and reduce the heat to a simmer. Simmer until the octopus is tender, about 2 hours. Be sure that the octopus is completely covered with water during the cooking time, and add more water if needed.

6 When the octopus is tender, remove it from the cooking liquid and place it, still wet, immediately in a loaf pan or terrine. Tuck in all of the tentacles and place another loaf pan or something that fits in the loaf pan directly on top of the octopus. Put a brick or several cans in the top loaf pan as weights. Refrigerate at least 24 hours. The octopus will keep up to a week if you are planning ahead.

7 To serve, remove the sliced onions from the red wine vinegar. (You can reuse the vinegar in other dressings or discard.)

8 Slice the octopus salami very thin and arrange on the arugula. Drizzle with the olive dressing and garnish with the pickled onion slices.

# CALAMARI *in* FORNO
## *Oven-Fried Squid*

I'm not a big believer in dieting, so I surprised myself when I came up with this dish for some waist-watching clients and liked it even better than fried calamari. It's become one of my signature dishes and I've been serving it for years now. My favorite way to eat it is with a dollop of butternut squash "dice" (page 196) on the side—the sweetness complements the squid perfectly—but the calamari are great on their own, too.

By the way, you'll have lots of leftover bread crumbs. Put them in a sealed container and keep them in your pantry. They'll stay fresh for up to three weeks and you can use them to sprinkle on oysters before baking, to top casseroles or broiled fish, or sauté some in lots of olive oil with garlic and red pepper flakes for a quick pasta sauce. **SERVES 4**

½ cup Bread Crumbs (page 27)

2 teaspoons finely chopped garlic

1½ teaspoons each of finely chopped fresh rosemary, thyme, sage, and oregano

1½ pounds squid, cleaned and cut into rings

¼ cup extra virgin olive oil

WINE SUGGESTION: *My first choice would be a San Angelo Pinot Grigio, which is fruity and good as an apéritif.*

1 Preheat the broiler.

2 Combine the bread crumbs, garlic, and herbs in a medium bowl.

3 In a separate bowl drizzle the squid with the olive oil and toss until all the rings are well coated.

4 Add the squid to the crumb mixture and stir gently until all the rings are coated.

5 Arrange the squid rings in a single layer on a nonstick baking sheet and broil for 3 to 4 minutes per side until lightly brown. Serve immediately.

# BREAD CRUMBS

MAKES 4 CUPS

1 loaf day-old Tuscan bread, cut into 1-inch cubes (Do not remove the crusts.)

5 teaspoons minced garlic

1 tablespoon finely chopped fresh thyme

3 tablespoons extra virgin olive oil

Salt

Freshly ground black pepper

1 Preheat the oven to 375° F.

2 Spread the bread cubes in a single even layer on a baking sheet. Bake until very crispy and dry, about 20 minutes, stirring occasionally to prevent burning and to make sure all the sides are toasted. Remove and let cool.

3 Working in small batches, place the cooled bread cubes in a food processor and pulse to fine crumbs.

4 Shake all the crumbs through a mesh strainer or sieve into a large bowl. This will filter out the larger pieces, making all the crumbs of uniform size.

5 Add the garlic, thyme, olive oil, and salt and pepper to taste. Using the palms of your hands, rub all of the ingredients together. The result should be very uniform, highly flavored bread crumbs.

# SEPPIE *in* ZIMINO
## *Cuttlefish with Cumin*

Cumin might not be the first spice you'd expect to find in a Tuscan kitchen, but it's been around forever, and we Tuscans especially like it for fish. Some people think the Germans who came to Tuscany in the seventeenth century introduced cumin to the area; others think it trickled up from southern Italy, where Arabic influence was strong. **SERVES 4 TO 6**

1½ cups roughly chopped onion

¾ cup roughly chopped carrots

1½ cups roughly chopped celery

2 garlic cloves

¼ cup extra virgin olive oil

Pinch crushed red pepper

2 tablespoons finely chopped fresh Italian parsley

1¾ pounds cleaned cuttlefish or squid, cut lengthwise into 1-inch strips

1 tablespoon ground cumin

1 cup dry white wine

Salt

Freshly ground black pepper

½ cup canned whole plum tomatoes with their juices, pureed or crushed with your hands (You can use canned pureed tomatoes, but I think the whole ones are less acidic and higher in quality.)

2 pounds Swiss chard, washed, stems cut into 1-inch lengths, and leaves chopped (16 cups)

1 cup vegetable stock or water

6 slices Tuscan bread, toasted and rubbed with raw garlic

**WINE SUGGESTION:** *There isn't a lot of Syrah grown in Italy, but I think Isole e Olena Syrah is a good bet with this dish. It has a little pepper to it, which compliments the cuttlefish.*

1  In a food processor puree the onion, carrots, celery, and garlic to a coarse paste.

2  Coat the bottom of a large skillet with the olive oil. Add the pureed vegetables, crushed red pepper, and parsley and sauté over medium heat for 10 to 15 minutes, or until the vegetables start to color. Add the cuttlefish, cumin, and wine. Season with salt and pepper, bring to a boil, and cook until the wine is reduced by half.

3  Add the tomatoes, Swiss chard, and vegetable stock or water and simmer for 25 to 30 minutes.

4  Taste for seasonings. To serve, spoon over the toasted garlic bread.

# SEPPIE *con* PISELLI

## *Cuttlefish with Green Peas*

I love cuttlefish for its chewy softness and the way sauces cling perfectly to it. Plus, cuttlefish has always been inexpensive. If you look in ledgers from the 1400s in Venice, for example, one hundred cuttlefish cost five *soldi*, while just one turbot cost four *soldi*. SERVES 4 TO 6

¼ cup extra virgin olive oil

1 tablespoon minced garlic, plus 1 whole clove

1 teaspoon crushed red pepper

2 tablespoons finely chopped fresh Italian parsley

1¾ pounds cleaned cuttlefish or calamari, cut into ½ inch rings

1 cup white wine

½ cup canned whole plum tomatoes, pureed or crushed (You can use canned pureed tomatoes, but I think the whole ones are less acidic and of better quality.)

2⅔ cups green peas, fresh or frozen (The frozen do not need to be cooked separately.)

Salt

Freshly ground black pepper

6 slices Tuscan bread

WINE SUGGESTION: *We usually make this dish at the beginning of summer when peas are at their sweetest. I like it with a light-bodied Vernaccia like Terre di Tufi, which comes from San Gimignano.*

1 Pour the olive oil into a large pan, add the garlic, crushed red pepper, and parsley, and sauté over medium heat until the garlic starts to color, about 5 minutes.

2 Add the cuttlefish, cover, and cook for 5 minutes.

3 Add the wine and cook until it has reduced by half, 5 to 10 minutes.

4 Add the tomatoes and peas and season with salt and pepper to taste. Simmer for 40 minutes. Add water if the mixture becomes dry.

5 Meanwhile, toast the bread slices and rub each slice with the remaining garlic clove.

6 Taste the cuttlefish for seasoning. To serve, spoon over the toasted garlic bread.

# SGOMBRO *con* PUREE *di* VERDURE *e* CECI

## *Mackerel with Vegetable Puree and Chick-Peas*

This is my interpretation of an old Roman recipe. I'm not sure what kinds of vegetables they would have used, but I take what I can find. The original version also included garum—a fermented fish sauce—and sometimes I throw in a few anchovies to approximate that flavor. I've omitted them here so that you can really taste the flavor of the fresh mackerel. **SERVES 4**

1 pound spinach or dandelion leaves, well washed (**If using spinach, trim the ribs to yield about 8 cups.**)

6 tablespoons extra virgin olive oil

½ cup finely chopped red onion

2 teaspoons minced garlic

Pinch crushed red pepper

½ cup dry white wine

2 cups cooked chick-peas (page 187) (**If using the canned variety, make sure to rinse them well.**)

Salt

Freshly ground black pepper

1 pound mackerel fillets, cut into 8 equal pieces, skin intact

---

**WINE SUGGESTION:** *Look for a big Chardonnay like I Sistri from Fattoria di Felsina to go with the oily mackerel.*

---

1 Bring a large pot of well-salted water to a boil. Add the greens and cook for 3 to 5 minutes. Drain and cool under cold water. Squeeze out the excess water and set aside.

2 Coat the bottom of a large skillet with 3 tablespoons of the olive oil. Add the onion, garlic, and crushed red pepper and sauté over medium heat for 5 minutes. Add the wine and 1 cup of the chick-peas and season with salt and pepper. Cook until the wine has reduced by half.

3 Add the greens and cook until all the moisture has evaporated, about 5 minutes.

4 Puree the greens and the sautéed chick-peas in a food processor until smooth and soupy. (If the puree is too thick, add a little water.) Pour into a saucepan and keep warm over low heat.

5 Season the mackerel with salt and pepper and rub with some of the remaining olive oil. Coat the bottom of a large skillet with the remaining oil, heat over high heat, and add the fillets. Sauté until the mackerel is cooked through, 2 to 3 minutes per side. (You can also grill the fish over high heat or broil it, but keep a close eye on it so that it doesn't burn.)

6 Ladle the puree over the bottom of a large soup plate or bowl. Arrange a small mound of the remaining chick-peas on the puree and lean the cooked mackerel pieces up against the chick-peas. Drizzle with extra virgin olive oil.

# CIORTONI *in* UMIDO *con* POLENTA
## *Mackerel with Polenta*

Italians use polenta to stretch a meal. In this bargain dinner, you're stretching mackerel, already one of the cheapest fish in the sea. Fishermen's families have eaten this combination forever, and when I was growing up, it was the first thing I'd order when my family went to eat at the seaside town of Viareggio. It might seem strange to think of polenta as a hot-weather ingredient, but it's made from summer corn after all. SERVES 6

1 cup flour

1 teaspoon salt

1 tablespoon crushed red pepper

1 pound mackerel fillets, cut in 2-inch pieces

1 cup peanut oil

1 tablespoon chopped garlic

2 tablespoons extra virgin olive oil

1 teaspoon minced fresh rosemary

1 teaspoon minced fresh Italian parsley

1 teaspoon minced fresh basil

1 teaspoon minced fresh sage

2 tablespoons chopped anchovy fillets (about 6) in oil (I prefer the taste of salted anchovies, but they need to be soaked in white wine or water for a few hours or overnight before using.)

¼ cup dry white wine

3½ cups canned whole tomatoes with their juice, crushed by hand (You can use crushed canned tomatoes, but I think the whole ones are less acidic and of better quality.)

2 ounces (2½ tablespoons) pitted black olives

8 cups hot cooked polenta (page 198)

---

WINE SUGGESTION: *Some of my favorite Italian whites come from near Massa Carrara, the mountaintop town most famous for its marble. I like either Vermentino made by the two local producers, Cima and Lambruschi.*

---

1 Stir the flour, salt, and crushed red pepper together in a bowl. Dredge the mackerel fillets in the mixture.

2 In a large skillet heat the peanut oil over high heat to 375°. Add the fish and fry 2 to 3 minutes on each side, until golden brown. Drain on paper towels.

3 In a separate skillet large enough to hold all the fish sauté the garlic in the olive oil until it starts to color. Add the rosemary, parsley, basil, sage, anchovies, and wine. (If you can't find all of the herbs, use those you can find.) Cook until the wine has reduced by half.

4 Add the tomatoes and ½ cup water. Cook for 5 minutes on medium-high heat, then add the mackerel and the olives and heat through. Serve over the polenta.

## • FRESH HERBS •

I'd like to say something about my lavish use of fresh herbs. If you've ever seen me in person or pictured in a newspaper article, you'll know that I almost never go anywhere without a bouquet of rosemary, sage, and thyme in my pocket. I have rows of herbs in front of Beppe, and back in Italy, the grounds of my family's restaurant, Vipore, was planted with everything from lemon thyme to bay trees to lemongrass. I'm an herb fanatic—and with reason. Fresh herbs have incredible aromatic oils that can transform even a dull piece of chicken into a memorable dinner. Dried herbs can't compare. Just try rubbing some fresh rosemary or sage between your fingers and smell them. Then try the same thing with dried herbs. You'll see what I mean.

I understand that it's not always easy to get lots of fresh herbs, so I suggest substituting another fresh herb, one that is easier to find, instead of using a dried alternative. A dish might not taste the same, but it can still be delicious. (Be sure to adjust amounts to reflect the different levels of intensity herbs have; basil, for example, is mild, while rosemary is strong.) If, in a worst case scenario, you have to use dried herbs, use about a third of the dried variety for the fresh amount. (One tablespoon fresh rosemary is the equivalent of about a teaspoon dried.) And replace your dried herbs regularly. That will take care of the biggest problem of all, which is letting bottled herbs sit on shelves for years, where they lose any of the little flavor they might have had when first jarred.

# SARDINE *con* PANCETTA *e* PARMESAN

## *Sardines with Bacon and Cheese*

Italians have always eaten a lot of seafood, not only because of its availability but also because up until 1965 the Church had Catholics eating fish on Fridays and throughout Lent. We followed that rule at our house, even after things loosened up. I always looked forward to Fridays because it meant a trip into town with my grandfather, who liked to eat the canned tuna and sardines served in bars back then, followed by a glass of wine. That was my first experience with sardines and even though I was little and the taste was strong, they stuck with me. When I started cooking, I made sardines the classic Italian way, just marinating fresh ones overnight in olive oil with lemon, salt, and red pepper. New Yorkers weren't so crazy about that preparation, though, so I switched to the approach below. Pancetta provides pork flavor and cuts the fishy flavor that people tend not to like. **SERVES** 8

3 tablespoons extra virgin olive oil

2 ounces pancetta or bacon, minced (½ cup)

1 cup seasoned Bread Crumbs (page 27)

2 tablespoons finely chopped fresh Italian parsley

2 teaspoons finely chopped fresh marjoram

3 tablespoons grated Parmesan cheese

¾ tablespoon grated lemon zest

Salt

Freshly ground black pepper

2 pounds fresh sardines, cleaned, scaled, gutted, deboned and butterflied

2 tablespoons lemon juice

---

**WINE SUGGESTION:** *Try a medium-bodied white like I Campetti l'Accesa Malvasia, which is nice and fragrant.*

---

1 Preheat the oven to 400° F. Lightly oil a cookie sheet with 1 tablespoon of the olive oil and set aside.

2 Coat the bottom of a small skillet with the remaining olive oil. Add the pancetta and sauté over medium heat until crispy and lightly browned. Remove from the skillet and set aside.

**3** On a large plate combine the bread crumbs, parsley, marjoram, Parmesan, lemon zest, salt and pepper to taste, and pancetta.

**4** Season the sardines with salt and pepper and sprinkle with the lemon juice.

**5** Place each sardine, skin side up, in the seasoned bread crumbs and press lightly to coat. Place the sardines crumb side up, on the cookie sheet. Bake for 5 to 7 minutes. When done, the sardines should be cooked through and the crumbs should be brown and crispy. Serve immediately with a mixed green salad.

## • SARDINES •

Sardines are a cheap fish, a fact that hasn't changed much since Roman times. Indeed, they've always been so plentiful around Italy that they gave Sardinia its name. Because of their strong flavor—they were an ingredient in garum, the powerful Roman fish sauce—sardines are usually sold canned in oil. Look for brands that use olive oil, a sign the sardines are of a higher grade. I'd also avoid any varieties that can sardines in a spicy or tomato sauce, since that seems to me another way to mask poorer quality. Above all, try sardines the way I like them—fresh from the market, then grilled with pancetta and bread crumbs.

One last thought: If you're cooking with canned sardines, do not bone them. The bones will dissolve and add calcium to the sauce.

# GAMBERONI *con* ARANCI *e* FINOCCHIO

## *Shrimp with Blood Orange and Fennel Salad*

Until recently in Italy, you never could have found an orange and fennel salad outside of Sicily, where sweet and sour is a local passion. But thanks in part to tourists who want Ligurian pesto when they're in Rome or risotto Milanese in Florence, our food regionalism is softening. To me, this salad is worth eating anywhere. I've seen cooks use it as a topping for salmon and pasta, but I prefer combining it with shrimp. If you can't find the dramatic blood oranges, any sweet variety will do. **SERVES 4 TO 6**

1½ pounds large shrimp, with shells

3 blood oranges (enough to make 3 cups orange sections)

1 teaspoon finely chopped fresh rosemary

1 scant tablespoon sliced garlic

1 tablespoon hot pepper sauce, such as Tabasco

4 tablespoons extra virgin olive oil

Salt

Freshly ground black pepper

1 fennel bulb, thinly sliced lengthwise (1½ cups)

1¼ cups thinly sliced celery

1½ cups leaves from celery hearts

2 tablespoons whole fresh Italian parsley leaves

2 tablespoons raspberry or other fruit vinegar

**WINE SUGGESTION:** *Add a spoonful of blood orange juice to a glass of a sparkling wine and you can't go wrong. Or, if you want to keep it simple, pick up a Vernaccia di San Gimignano, such as La Gentilesca.*

1  Cut the shrimp in half lengthwise, keeping the shell and tail intact.

2  Using a sharp knife, cut off both the top and bottom of the blood oranges. Remove the skin and the pith (the white part) from the outside of each orange. Carefully cut in between the segments to remove the flesh of the orange without any membranes. Work over a bowl to collect the juices. Place all of the segments in a strainer set over the bowl to collect the juices.

**3** In a large bowl combine the shrimp, rosemary, garlic, hot pepper sauce, 1 tablespoon of the olive oil, and salt and pepper to taste. Toss well, cover with plastic, and let stand for 1 hour on the counter or up to 24 hours in the refrigerator.

**4** Put the fennel, celery, celery leaves, and parsley in another large bowl. Cover with 4 cups of ice water, stir in 1 tablespoon salt, and refrigerate for at least 30 minutes but no longer than 24 hours. This will keep the fennel and celery crisp and prevent them from turning brown.

**5** To make the blood orange vinaigrette: Combine the collected blood orange juice, about 3 tablespoons, with the raspberry vinegar. Whisking constantly, slowly add 3 tablespoons of the remaining olive oil. Season with salt and pepper and set aside.

**6** Preheat the broiler or grill to its highest setting.

**7** When ready to assemble the salad, remove the fennel, celery, celery leaves, and parsley from the ice water and pat dry. Remove the shrimp from the marinade and grill, shell side down, until cooked through, 5 to 7 minutes. If broiling, place the shrimp shell upside down on a sizzle platter or baking sheet on a rack 5 inches from the heat. Move the pan every few minutes until the shrimp are ready, 5 to 10 minutes, depending how hot the broiler is.

**8** Toss the fennel mixture with the orange segments and the blood orange vinaigrette. Arrange the salad on individual plates, distribute the shrimp evenly on top, and serve.

# TRIGLIE *con* MELANZANE *e* POMODORO

## *Red Mullet with Eggplant and Tomatoes*

It's hard to get out of Livorno without eating some type of red mullet—a little like going to Maryland and skipping the crab. Locals prefer the rock variety, which is a beautiful metallic red, over the sand mullet, which is bigger, pink, and has softer flesh. The classic way to eat mullet is pan fried, but I like how my friend Franca Franceschini, the chef at Romano's in Viareggio, does rock mullet, so I copied her. **SERVES 4**

Salt

4 cups peeled diced eggplant

5 tablespoons extra virgin olive oil

1 tablespoon minced garlic

1 tablespoon finely chopped fresh Italian parsley

Pinch crushed red pepper

½ cup dry white wine

2 cups peeled, seeded, and diced fresh tomatoes

2 tablespoons sliced basil leaves

Freshly ground black pepper

1½ pounds red mullet (4 fish), filleted and tiny pinbones removed (ask your fishmonger to do this)

---

**WINE SUGGESTION:** *It's not a traditional match, but I like a rosé here: the color complements the blush of the fish. Any light red would do well, too, such as a Fattoria di Felsina Chianti.*

---

1 Salt the eggplant well and put it in a colander. Place a plate or heavy weight on top and let it drain for 45 minutes to 1 hour.

2 Preheat the oven to 375° F.

3 Coat the bottom of a large skillet with 3 tablespoons of the olive oil. Add the garlic, parsley, and crushed red pepper and sauté over medium heat until the garlic starts to color.

4 Add the wine and reduce by half.

5  Add the tomatoes, basil, eggplant, and ½ cup water and season well with salt and pepper. Cook over high heat until the eggplant is very soft and the liquid has almost totally evaporated, 15 to 20 minutes. Transfer the eggplant mixture to a 10- by 13-inch ovenproof dish and spread in a thin even layer.

6  Season the mullet with salt and pepper and rub with the remaining 2 tablespoons olive oil. Arrange the fish on the eggplant mixture. Bake until the fish is cooked through, 7 to 10 minutes. Transfer to a serving platter.

# POLPETTE *di* MERLUZZO

## *Cod Cakes*

Cod found an early proponent in Italy in the sixteenth-century pontiff, Pope Pius V, father of the city of Pienza. Once Pius's favorite recipes were collected into a cookbook, his preferred dishes, including cod, quickly spread to other towns. The cake shape isn't a traditional way to eat cod in Italy—especially with a chipotle pepper in the sauce—but I was inspired to make cod cakes after discovering crab cakes in America. (I love the smoky flavor from the chipotle.) If you want a more classic Tuscan flavor, substitute a good pinch of cayenne pepper for the chipotle, and if you want a shortcut, use 3 cups of mayonnaise instead of making the sauce recipe with eggs and peanut oil. In that case, you will need to reduce the vinegar to 1 teaspoon.

**SERVES 8 AS AN APPETIZER**

### THE SAUCE

1 jalapeño pepper, seeds removed

1 teaspoon red wine vinegar

1 egg

½ chipotle pepper in adobo sauce with 1 teaspoon of the sauce

2 teaspoons Dijon mustard

1½ teaspoons finely chopped fresh Italian parsley

Salt

Freshly ground black pepper

1½ cups peanut oil

---

**WINE SUGGESTION:** *Conventional wisdom has it you're supposed to drink white wine with fish, but every time I eat this dish I want a spicy Syrah. Try Colvecchio from Castello Banfi.*

---

### THE COD CAKES

1 small red onion, cut in half

1 carrot, halved

1 celery stalk, halved

2 whole garlic cloves

1 bay leaf

1 pound skinless boneless fresh cod

¾ cup cubed day-old bread, crusts removed, plus 1 cube

¼ cup extra virgin olive oil

½ cup finely diced red onion

2 teaspoons minced garlic

½ cup diced leek (white part only)

¾ cup finely diced red bell pepper

6 ounces oyster mushrooms (shiitake or button mushrooms are also acceptable)

¼ cup whiskey, scotch, or bourbon

1 tablespoon whole-grain mustard

¼ cup heavy cream

½ cup Bread Crumbs (page 27)

2 eggs

2 tablespoons lemon juice

½ to 1 cup peanut oil for frying

1 For the sauce: Put the seeded jalapeño pepper, red wine vinegar, the eggs, chipotle pepper and sauce, mustard, parsley, salt, and pepper in a food processor and puree for 1 minute.

2 Add the peanut oil in a thin, slow stream. Stop when you've put in about 2 cups of the oil, taste for seasoning, then continue adding the remaining 1 cup oil. The consistency should be like mayonnaise. Refrigerate until ready to use.

3 For the cod cakes: Combine the onion halves, carrot, celery, whole garlic cloves, bay leaf and cod in a large saucepan, cover with water, and season with salt and pepper. Bring to a simmer and cook for 5 to 10 minutes, or until the fish is cooked through. Remove the cod from the water and set aside to cool.

4 Place the bread cubes in a bowl and moisten with water. Set aside.

5 Coat the bottom of a large skillet with the olive oil. Add the diced onion, minced garlic, leeks, red pepper, and mushrooms and sauté over medium heat until the vegetables are soft, 10 to 15 minutes. Season with salt and pepper.

6 Add the whiskey, mustard, and heavy cream and cook until the liquid has completely evaporated. Remove the pan from the heat and let cool.

7 In a large bowl combine the sautéed vegetable mixture, the cooked cod, the bread crumbs, the remaining 2 eggs, and lemon juice.

*(continued)*

8   Squeeze the excess water out of the bread and add the bread to the cod mixture. Season with salt and pepper. Using your hand or a wooden spoon, combine well; the cod will break up into small flakes. The mixture should be fairly smooth and homogeneous.

9   Form the mixture into 8 3- to 4-inch cakes, cover with plastic wrap, and refrigerate at least ½ an hour and no more than 24 hours until ready to cook.

10   Pour the peanut oil into a large skillet to a depth of about ⅛ inch and heat over medium heat. (Test the temperature: When the remaining cube of bread sizzles when dropped in the oil, the oil is hot enough for frying. Do not leave the bread in the oil.) Add as many cod cakes as will fit comfortably in the pan and brown to crispy on both sides. You will need to cook the cakes in batches. Drain on paper towels. Keep the cooked cakes in a warm spot near the oven. Serve with the sauce.

# CECINA

## *Chick-Pea Flatbread*

I am a huge fan of chick-peas, but even if I weren't I'd have to respect them for their pedigree. To start with, the pea's botanical name, *Cicer arietinum,* was inspired by the Greek myths (the pea is shaped like Aries, the ram's head), and the Roman orator and statesman Cicero got his name from the chick-pea-sized wart on his nose. Then there are the Sicilians. When they rebelled against the French in 1282, they identified—and killed—foreigners who pronounced chick-pea the French way.

*Cecina,* a chick-pea flour flatbread, is especially popular in Liguria. *Cecina* is served in pizzerias, and when I was growing up my dad used to take me to a place after school for a slice. I didn't like it at first, but over time I grew to love the sweet dough and the tangy black pepper sprinkled on top. **SERVES 6**

1⅓ cups plus 2 tablespoons chick-pea flour (available in Indian markets or health food stores)

½ cup extra virgin olive oil

2 teaspoons coarse salt

Freshly ground black pepper

**WINE SUGGESTION:** *This snack calls for a crisp, fresh white. In Lucca, we almost always pair* cecina *with the locally made Sauvignon Terre di Sibolla, but your favorite Sauvignon will work just as well.*

1 Preheat the oven to 425° F.

2 Mound the chick-pea flour in a large bowl and make a well in it.

3 Pour in ¼ cup of the olive oil, 2 cups water, and the salt. Combine with a whisk until smooth. (The mixture should look like very thin pancake batter.) Let the batter rest for 20 to 30 minutes on the countertop.

4 Pour 1 tablespoon of the remaining olive oil into each of two 6-inch square cast-iron pans. Pour in the batter and drizzle the remaining 2 tablespoons olive oil on top. Sprinkle the batter with freshly ground black pepper.

5 Bake the *cecina* on the middle rack until set and a deep golden brown, 25 to 35 minutes. Check periodically to make sure it is cooking evenly.

6 Remove the pans from the oven. Run a paring knife along the edges to loosen the breads, release them with a long spatula run underneath, and turn them out onto a cutting board. Let rest a few minutes. Slice into bars or wedges and serve.

# FOCACCIA

## *Focaccia*

I know it's inevitable for foods to change and evolve, but the way focaccia has been treated in the United States just isn't a good thing. Instead of the perfect slice—somewhere between crispy and soft, drizzled with olive oil, and sprinkled with lots of salt—focaccia here has become a gummy mess, smothered with onions and tomato sauce. After all, even without fancy ovens, the Romans who came up with the recipe managed to get it right. At least I think they did as we kept the name they gave it (*focaccia* is derived from the Latin *focus* meaning hearth) and still eat it the way they did, with our hands. I like sage and rosemary worked into the dough, but you can be even more of a purist than I am and leave them out.

**SERVES 4 TO 6, YIELD: 1¼ LBS**

1 ounce active dry yeast

1 teaspoon sugar

1½ cups warm water

4 cups unbleached flour

2 tablespoons extra virgin olive oil, plus more for drizzling

2 teaspoons minced garlic

2 teaspoons salt, plus more to taste

½ teaspoon freshly ground black pepper, plus more to taste

2 tablespoons finely chopped fresh rosemary

6 tablespoons finely chopped fresh sage

4 tablespoons butter, melted (optional)

1  In a large mixing bowl combine the yeast, sugar, water and ½ cup of the flour and mix well. (This can be done with a wooden spoon or in a food processor or standing electric mixer. A handheld electric mixer is not strong enough to handle the job.)

2  Add the olive oil, garlic, salt, pepper, herbs, optional melted butter, and remaining 3½ cups flour. Work the ingredients together until the dough is smooth and firm. Wrap the dough loosely in plastic wrap, put it in a warm place, and allow to rise for 1½ hours.

**3** After the dough has risen, punch it down and stretch it out on a very well oiled baking sheet. Drizzle a generous amount of olive oil over the dough. Work the dough with the tips of your fingers to make dimples all over the surface. Cover the baking sheet loosely with plastic wrap and allow the dough to rise again until it has doubled in size, about 45 minutes.

**4** Preheat the oven to 400° F.

**5** Sprinkle the dough with salt and pepper. Bake for 5 minutes, then lower the oven temperature to 350° and bake for an additional 30 minutes. Focaccia is best eaten hot. Serve immediately. If you don't eat it all immediately, store it in a brown paper bag at room temperature and reheat (out of the bag) the next day.

# CROSTINI *con* PUREE *di* FAGIOLI

## *Tuscan Bean Puree on Toast*

In Tuscany, we use bean puree only in soups like *zuppa di gran farro*, but I invented this puree as a kind of Tuscan hummus minus the tahini. When I make it, I do it in small quantities; otherwise I snack on the puree so much that there's barely any left for my guests. To dress this antipasto up, use small toast rounds instead of slices of bread; rub them with a garlic clove, spread a little of the puree on each round, and top each off with a boiled shrimp or a teaspoon of caviar. **YIELD: ABOUT 3 CUPS**

3–6 cloves garlic, or more if desired

¼ cup extra virgin olive oil

2 cups cooked white beans (page 187, cooking water reserved)

2 tablespoons chopped fresh Italian parsley

Pinch grated nutmeg

Salt

Freshly ground black pepper

10–12 slices grilled or toasted Tuscan bread (or any other crusty peasant bread or toast rounds), rubbed with raw garlic

**WINE SUGGESTION:** *The spicy berry flavor of Lagone by Aia Vecchia is a nice complement to the creamy puree.*

1 Preheat the oven to 375° F.

2 In a small baking dish toss the garlic cloves with the olive oil. Roast in the oven until soft, 15 to 20 minutes.

3 In a food processor puree the roasted garlic with its oil. Add the beans with ¼ cup of the bean cooking water and pulse until a coarse paste has formed. Add more liquid if needed. This mixture should not be smooth.

4 Add the parsley, nutmeg, and salt and pepper to taste and pulse until well combined. Adjust the seasoning if needed. Serve at room temperature with warm grilled garlic-rubbed Tuscan bread.

# FRITTATA *di* ZOCCOLE

## *Potato and Egg Frittata*

When I was little, I used to sneak into my grandma's chicken coop, poke a hole in the eggs, and suck out the insides. Then I'd put the eggs back. After a few weeks, everyone was talking about the beast that was sucking the eggs dry—until my father blew my cover. How did he know it was me? He used to do the same thing when he was little.

Even in Italy, eggs aren't that fresh anymore, but they're still about the cheapest protein around—hence the volume of frittata recipes in Tuscany. The *zoccole*, which translates as clogs, is slang for the chunks of pancetta that give the frittata its zip. **SERVES** 6

7 tablespoons extra virgin olive oil

2 ounces pancetta, minced (½ cup)

1 pound potatoes, boiled, peeled, and cut into ½-inch slices (3 cups)

2½ cups sliced onions

1 teaspoon finely chopped fresh thyme

Salt

Freshly ground black pepper

9 eggs

2 tablespoons grated Parmesan cheese

**WINE SUGGESTION:** *Look for wines from around Lucca that are made with the Sangiovese grape. One of our most popular table wines at Beppe is Rosso delle Colline Lucchesi, a medium-bodied red that is the color of rubies.*

1 Preheat the oven to 375° F.

2 Coat the bottom of a large skillet with 3 tablespoons of the olive oil. Add the pancetta and sauté over medium heat until crisp. Add the potatoes and cook for 3 to 5 minutes, or until browned. Add the onions, thyme, and salt and pepper to taste and cook for 5 minutes. Set aside to cool.

3 In a large bowl beat the eggs with salt and pepper and the Parmesan. Stir in the potato and pancetta mixture and combine well.

4 Coat the bottom of a large ovenproof skillet with the remaining 4 tablespoons olive oil and heat over medium heat. Pour in the egg and potato mixture.

5 Transfer the skillet to the oven and bake for 10 to 12 minutes, or until the center of the frittata has set.

6 Turn the fritatta out onto a large plate or platter and serve immediately or let cool and serve at room temperature.

# FRITTATA *di* FAGIOLI

## *Bean Frittata*

If you believe that frittatas and omelets are the same thing, don't tell that to an Italian. First of all, we've been making frittatas in Tuscany since at least the 1400s, when Giovanni di Cosimo de' Medici had his cook make them for guests. Secondly, frittatas are cooked at a much lower heat and for a longer time than omelets and are meant to be substantial and firm, not fluffy or runny. You might think it odd to combine eggs and beans, but for me each bean is like those nuggets of chocolate in a quart of vanilla ice cream: I love digging them out one by one. SERVES 4

6 eggs

¼ cup freshly grated Parmesan cheese

Salt

Freshly ground pepper

2 tablespoons extra virgin olive oil

1 teaspoon minced garlic

1 tablespoon chopped fresh sage

Pinch crushed red pepper

1½ cups cooked cannellini or great northern beans (page 187), or use canned beans, rinsed well

WINE SUGGESTION: *You can't go wrong with Castello Banfi Serena Sauvignon Blanc, which is full and soft and perfect with this dish.*

1 Preheat the oven to 375° F.

2 In a bowl combine the eggs and Parmesan. Beat only to break up the egg yolks. Season with salt and pepper. Set aside.

3 Coat a large nonstick ovenproof skillet with the olive oil. Add the garlic, sage, and crushed red pepper and heat over medium heat.

4 When the garlic begins to color, add the beans. Stir to coat with the oil and season with salt and pepper.

5 Pour in the egg mixture and stir to incorporate the beans throughout. When the edges of the eggs begin to set, transfer the skillet to the oven. Bake for 10 to 15 minutes, or until the eggs are firm. Turn the frittata out of the pan onto a large plate or platter and serve immediately or let cool and serve at room temperature.

# FRITTATA *di* RICOTTA
## *Ricotta Frittata*

The best ricotta is a farmer's jewel—thick, tangy, and, contrary to health regulations, unpasteurized. But we eat it anyway, at room temperature with a spoon, like kids skimming cream off the top of milk. Around Garfagnana, the mountain town where my mom grew up, this frittata is a staple, but is never served as an individual dish; the frittatas they made were huge and were sliced into single servings. You can't beat it for a buffet. It's also great with tomato sauce on top. Make sure to use the highest quality ricotta you can find. SERVES 4

3 tablespoons olive oil, plus more for drizzling

½ cup sliced onions

1 teaspoon chopped, fresh marjoram

Salt

Freshly ground black pepper

6 eggs

¾ cup ricotta cheese

3 tablespoons grated Parmesan cheese

WINE SUGGESTION: *With ricotta, I like a rich Chardonnay. Avignonesi Marzocco is a good choice.*

1 Preheat the oven to 375° F.

2 Coat the bottom of a large ovenproof skillet with the olive oil. Add the onions, marjoram, and salt and pepper to taste and sauté over medium heat until the onions are translucent and very aromatic, 5 to 7 minutes.

3 In a bowl combine the eggs, ricotta, and Parmesan and stir until smooth and homogeneous.

4 Add the egg mixture to the sautéed onions and stir to incorporate the onions. Cook the frittata on the stovetop until the eggs start to set, then transfer the skillet to the oven. Bake for 12 to 15 minutes, or until firm.

5 Turn the frittata out of the pan onto a large serving plate. Drizzle with olive oil if desired and serve immediately. Or let cool and serve at room temperature.

# INSALATA *di* POLLO
## *Chicken Salad*

For some reason, no one thinks of chicken salad as an Italian dish, but it's been part of the Italian table since Roman times. Apicius had a version that was packed with just about every herb and condiment in the pantry: celery seed, dried mint, ginger, coriander, raisins, and honey, not to mention oil, vinegar, and wine. There was a heartier version with bits of bread layered with chicken and sweetbreads, but since the bread was made with fermented semolina, it would probably be a little strong for the modern palate. I like serving this chicken salad, either cold or at room temperature, at a party. On a separate note, if you make your own stock for poaching the chicken, don't forget that it can make a great snack or even a light dinner after a day of overindulging. I like to add ginger, lemongrass, and jalapeño to the pot to give it kick. And, of course, you can't beat risotto made with homemade broth. **SERVES 4**

¼ cup dark raisins

½ cup dry white wine

1 quart Chicken Stock (page 66) (or good-quality canned broth)

Salt

1 pound boneless skinless chicken meat, both dark and white

⅓ cup finely chopped or grated carrots

⅓ cup finely chopped or grated celery

⅓ cup pine nuts, toasted

¼ cup lemon juice

3 tablespoons red wine vinegar

1 tablespoon minced fresh chives

1 teaspoon finely chopped fresh tarragon leaves

¼ cup extra virgin olive oil

Freshly ground black pepper

½ cup peeled and sliced tart apple, such as Granny Smith

1 head Boston lettuce or 2 cups mesclun

---

**WINE SUGGESTION:** *I could go with either a Chardonnay or a Pinot Grigio with this salad, but why not try Le Rime, which is a blend of both grapes and is nice and fruity.*

---

1  Combine the raisins and the wine. Set aside.

2  In a medium saucepan bring the chicken stock to a boil. Season well with salt. Add the chicken and simmer until cooked through, about 10 minutes. Turn off the heat and let the chicken cool in the stock.

3  In a large bowl combine the carrots, celery, pine nuts, lemon juice, vinegar, and herbs.

4  Drain the raisins, discarding the wine, and press the raisins to remove as much wine as possible. Add to the carrot mixture.

5  Shred the chicken and add it to the bowl. Drizzle in the olive oil and season well with salt and pepper. Toss well to combine and add the apples.

6  Arrange the lettuce on a platter and spoon the salad on top.

# PRIMI PIATTI
## Soups, Pastas, and Risotto

Growing up, I loved the legend about Marco Polo bringing pasta to Italy. Unfortunately, he didn't have anything to do with it. According to historians, the Arabs or the Etruscans may have been responsible. Since I'm partial to the Etruscans, who vanished from central Italy before the Romans arrived, I favor that theory. Famously inventive craftsmen, the Etruscans left behind detailed murals showing tools for producing pasta, including a wheel cutter like the one we use today to make fluted edges for pappardelle or tagliatelle. In one mural in Lazio outside of Rome, there's even an image of some chefs rolling out pasta as they're serenaded by a flute player.

On the other hand, pasta was well known in the Arab world, too. In the twelfth century, dried pasta was made commercially in Sicily, then an Arab colony. In fact, Palermo was the first historical capital of pasta, and noodles of different shapes were made there industrially, on a small scale.

One of my earliest memories is learning from my grandma how to hand roll *tordelli*, a traditional filled pasta from Lucca. I can still practically do it in my sleep, but nowadays I prefer to spend time inventing sauces instead of making pasta itself. I often look to history and tradition for inspiration. A "new" pasta dish that I'm obsessed with is Bengodi, a recipe inspired by the Boccaccio novel, *Decameron*, where disks of pasta roll down a mountain made of Parmesan into the fictional town of Bengodi. The locals then cook the pasta in capon broth. My dish: quarter-sized rounds of pasta, in a light bath of chicken broth, with lots of Parmesan and ground black pepper.

While many Americans think of a *primo piatto* as a pasta dish, the term also includes other starters, like soups, frittatas, and salads. In fact, *primi* can encompass a wide variety of dishes just as long as the portion size is small enough so that the diner will want to go on to the next course. In this chapter, I run through some of my favorite old and "new" classic *primi*. They're not trendy, and they're anything but fussy, but most are easy to make and excellent to eat.

# ZUPPA *di* FARRO

## *Farro Soup*

Although a handful of American restaurants have discovered farro, it is not so easy to find this ancient grain outside of Lucca, where I was born, and the absolute best variety comes from Garfagnana, where my mom grew up. I think of this *zuppa* as the Tuscan version of chicken soup: It cures all ills. And I believe it when locals say one hundred kernels of farro give you all the energy you need for a day. (The Romans must have thought the same: They paid their soldiers in spelt, or what we call *farro* or *emmer*.) The key to cooking spelt is water. Don't stint. It absorbs lots of water as it softens, and you want those grains as plump as possible. **SERVES 8**

**WINE SUGGESTION:** *Frescobaldi makes a big Merlot-based red called Giramonte, which some people might say is too strong for this dish, but I like it.*

1 cup quick-soaked dried cranberry beans (page 187)

2 small onions, 1 cut in half, 1 coarsely chopped

2 carrots, 1 whole, 1 coarsely chopped

2 stalks celery, 1 broken in half, 1 coarsely chopped

1 bay leaf

1 pound potatoes, peeled and cut into ½-inch dice (3 cups)

Salt

1⅓ cups farro (also called spelt, available in health food stores)

2 teaspoons chopped garlic

½ cup coarsely chopped leek, white part only

4 ounces pancetta, coarsely chopped (1 cup)

1 teaspoon finely chopped fresh sage leaves

1 teaspoon finely chopped fresh rosemary

½ teaspoon crushed red pepper

¼ cup extra virgin olive oil, plus more for drizzling

1 cup finely diced, peeled, and seeded butternut squash

¼ cup tomato paste

½ cup dry white wine

¼ cup grated Parmesan cheese, for serving

Freshly ground black pepper, for serving

1  To start the soup: Drain the beans and return them to the pot. Add the onion halves, the whole carrot, the whole celery stalk, the bay leaf, and potatoes. Add enough fresh water to cover the beans by at least 3 or 4 inches, bring to a simmer, and cook until the beans are soft. Depending on how old the beans are, this could take from 2 to 3 hours. Five minutes before removing from the heat, add salt. Rinse farro and cover, place in a large bowl and cover it with 3 cups cold water. Set aside.

2  With a slotted spoon, remove the beans and potatoes from the cooking liquid. Discard the onion, carrot, celery, and bay leaf, but reserve the liquid. Remove ¼ of the beans and potatoes and set aside.

3  In a food processor puree the remaining bean/potato mixture with the reserved cooking liquid. Set aside.

4  In the food processor puree the garlic, the chopped onion, chopped carrot, and chopped celery, the leek, pancetta, sage, rosemary, and crushed red pepper to a coarse paste.

5  Coat the bottom of a large stockpot with the ¼ cup olive oil. Add the pureed vegetable mixture and butternut squash and sauté over medium heat until the mixture starts to color, 10 to 15 minutes. Stir frequently to prevent sticking.

6  Add the tomato paste and wine and cook until the wine has reduced by half.

7  Add the bean puree and 1 quart water, season with salt and pepper, and simmer for 25 to 30 minutes, stirring occasionally to prevent sticking.

8  Drain the farro and add it to the soup. Add the reserved beans and potatoes and continue to cook for 40 to 45 minutes, adding 1 quart more water. If the soup becomes dry toward the end of the cooking time, add a little more water. Adjust the seasonings.

9  To serve, drizzle the soup with olive oil and sprinkle with the Parmesan and black pepper.

# ZUPPA *di* PATATE
## *Potato Soup*

It's so interesting to me to observe how perceptions of food evolve. When potatoes first arrived in Italy in the 1600s, they were so ugly people thought they carried leprosy and refused to eat them. History changed that of course (spurred by food shortages) and over time potatoes slowly worked their way into the Italian diet, in everything from gnocchi to this hearty peasant soup. Don't skimp on the croutons here; they're my favorite part. **SERVES 4**

1½ cups roughly chopped onions

1 cup roughly chopped carrots

2 cups roughly chopped celery

2 tablespoons roughly chopped garlic

3 ounces coarsely chopped pancetta (¾ cup)

Pinch crushed red pepper

¼ cup fresh Italian parsley leaves

¼ cup extra virgin olive oil, plus more for drizzling

½ cup dry white wine

2 cups canned tomatoes, drained and crushed

Salt

Freshly ground black pepper

4½ pounds Idaho potatoes, peeled and diced (13–14 cups)

1 tablespoon basil chiffonade

4 slices day-old bread, toasted, rubbed with raw garlic, and cut into cubes

¼ cup grated Parmesan cheese, for serving

WINE SUGGESTION: *Serve this rustic dish with a simple Chianti, or if you prefer a white, a Chardonnay like Fabrizio Bianchi from the Castello di Monsanto vineyard.*

1  In a food processor puree the onions, carrots, celery, garlic, pancetta, crushed red pepper, and parsley leaves to a coarse paste.

2  Coat the bottom of a stockpot with the ¼ cup olive oil. Add the pureed vegetable mixture and sauté over medium heat until the mixture starts to color, 10 to 15 minutes. Stir frequently to prevent sticking.

**3** Add the wine and reduce by half.

**4** Add the tomatoes and cook for 10 minutes. Season with salt and pepper.

**5** Add the potatoes and 3 quarts water. Bring to a simmer and cook for 45 minutes, or until the potatoes are very soft.

**6** Pass the soup through a food mill and return it to the stockpot. Cook for 15 minutes, adjust the seasonings, and add the basil.

**7** To serve, top the soup with the croutons, drizzle with a little olive oil, and sprinkle with the Parmesan and black pepper.

# ZUPPA di RICOTTA
## Ricotta Soup

It's not part of anyone's marketing campaign, but ricotta is made with the leftovers or whey of other cheeses, like pecorino or mozzarella. In fact, the word *ricotta* means recooked, and the kind I like best is unpasturized, sold directly from the shepherd. (You can't buy it this way—it's illegal and can be dangerous to eat—but it's delicious.) Back when only peasants ate ricotta, this soup was considered the most simple and humble a dish, but now that good ricotta is as pricey as aged pecorino, people go crazy for it. To me, it's the quintessential comfort food. SERVES 6

1 cup roughly chopped carrots

2 cups roughly chopped celery

1½ cups roughly chopped onions

1½ tablespoons sliced garlic

3 tablespoons extra virgin olive oil, plus more for drizzling

1 cup canned plum tomatoes, drained and pureed

3 cups roughly chopped fresh spinach (or 1 cup cooked frozen spinach)

Salt

Freshly ground black pepper

2 cups ricotta cheese

Pinch grated nutmeg

2 quarts water or vegetable stock

4 slices day-old bread, toasted, rubbed with garlic, and cut into cubes

½ cup grated pecorino cheese, for serving

---

WINE SUGGESTION: *I want a sweet, perfumed wine here, similar to the taste sensation of drizzling honey on ricotta for dessert. Think about a Viognier, like Almabruna.*

---

1 In a food processor puree the carrots, celery, onions, and garlic to a coarse paste.

2 Coat the bottom of a stockpot with the olive oil. Add the pureed vegetable mixture and sauté over medium heat until the mixture starts to color, 10 to 15 minutes. Stir frequently to prevent sticking.

3 Add the tomatoes, and spinach, and cook for 5 minutes. Season with salt and pepper.

4 Add the ricotta and stir to combine. Season with the nutmeg.

5 Add the water or vegetable stock and cook for 30 minutes. Adjust the seasonings.

6 To serve, divide the soup among 6 bowls, top each with cubes of the toasted bread, sprinkle with the pecorino and pepper, and drizzle with olive oil.

## • PLATINA AND MAESTRO MARTINO •

I think of Platina as a sort of Latin Elizabeth David. A fifteenth-century food buff, he loved to eat. He was the Vatican librarian, as well as a poet. In addition, Platina wrote the definitive book about how Italians ate back then, *Honest Pleasure and Good Health*. The volume recorded everything: the way people wrapped their flatware in napkins, recipes for zabaglione, natural cures for digestive problems. I love spending an afternoon reading the old recipes and have even adapted a few.

As useful as it is, though, there's something odd about Platina's book. The first five chapters run along smoothly enough, talking about good food, daily life, and agriculture. Then all of a sudden, it's just straight recipes. This section comes from Maestro Martino, a personal chef who had written his own book, *The Book of Cooking Arts*, with all the recipes of the era. (While he wasn't Tuscan, Martino lived in Tuscany, so I feel as if I have a connection to him.) Platina discovered the Martino manuscript while working at the Vatican and was so taken by it he just appropriated it into his own volume. I have no idea of Platina's motives since he was an expert in his own right, but thanks to the recipes by Martino, *Honest Pleasure* is considered the first published cookbook written by a chef on record. That said, it runs a close race with the first book by the famous French chef Taillevent, which it seems took longer to be published.

# CARABACCIA

## *Onion Soup*

Renaissance cookbooks reveal that onion soup was a staple for early Italian chefs like Cristoforo Messisburgo. And earlier still, there are references to onion soup in cookbooks from the 1300s. In some areas of Tuscany, almonds were added, or peas in the spring, and even eggs to give the dish more protein. The dish takes its name from the Greek *karabos*, which is a boat in the shape of a nutshell and refers to the tureen once used to serve the soup. The Romans didn't have onions to make onion soup, but they did use the *karabos*, a reminder of the influence of ancient Greece on Roman cooking. **SERVES 4 TO 6**

⅓ cup extra virgin olive oil, plus more as needed

2 ounces pancetta or prosciutto, diced (½ cup) (optional)

2 pounds sliced red onions (12 cups)

Salt

2 cups roughly chopped celery

1 cup roughly cut carrots

1 tablespoon roughly chopped garlic

½ teaspoon crushed red pepper

1 cup dry white wine

1½ quarts vegetable stock or water

1½ cups peas, fresh or frozen

Freshly ground black pepper

6 eggs

2 tablespoons white wine vinegar

6 slices Tuscan bread (or any crusty peasant-style loaf)

¼ cup grated Parmesan or pecorino cheese, for serving

---

**WINE SUGGESTION:** *I think the sweet onions here need a mellow red, like a light Merlot or a Chianti. I'd choose Centine, which is made with Sangiovese and Cabernet grapes.*

---

1  Coat the bottom of a stockpot with the ⅓ cup olive oil. Add the pancetta or prosciutto if using and brown lightly. Remove from the pan and set aside.

2  Add the onions and sauté over low heat until very soft and golden brown. This will take about 25 minutes. Don't rush this as slow cooking is what develops the onion flavor. Season with salt.

3  While the onions are cooking, puree the celery, carrots, and garlic in a food processor to a coarse paste.

4  Add the pureed vegetable mixture and crushed red pepper to the onions and sauté until soft and very aromatic.

5  Add the wine and cook until reduced by half. Return the pancetta or prosciutto to the pot.

6  Add the vegetable stock or water and simmer for 1 hour.

7  Add the peas and cook for 30 minutes. Add salt and pepper to taste.

8  In a small saucepan bring 2 cups salted water and the vinegar to a boil. Reduce the heat until no bubbles break the surface of the water. Crack 2 of the eggs into the water and cook for 4 minutes. With a spoon gently remove the eggs from the water and reserve in a shallow dish with enough fresh water to cover the eggs (this rinses off the vinegar and stops the cooking). Bring the water back to a boil and repeat this process until all of the eggs are poached.

9  Preheat the broiler.

10  Toast the slices of bread under the broiler. Brush with olive oil and sprinkle with the grated cheese. Return to the broiler until the cheese has melted.

11  Lay a slice of toast in the bottom of each of 6 ovenproof soup bowls, top with a poached egg, and ladle in some of the onion soup. Sprinkle the bowls with cheese, drizzle with olive oil, and place under the broiler to brown the cheese.

# ACQUACOTTA
## *Maremma Vegetable Soup*

To think, mosquitoes helped create this dish. Though it's been drained and cleaned up now, in the early 1900s, the southern Tuscan seaside area called Maremma was mostly swamp and had a huge malaria problem. To keep the mosquitoes away, locals loaded garlic and onions into all kinds of dishes, including this soup, throwing in whatever else was on hand, from herbs and grasses picked from the field to rabbit and vegetables. To me, *acquacotta* is as Tuscan as you can get—a reflection of our ability to get by on very little. In fact, the name means "cooked water," and in lean times, it's not much more than that, just a simple vegetable broth. You can also add chicken, beef, or fish. If you use fish, poach it right in the soup. SERVES 4 TO 6

¼ cup extra virgin olive oil, plus more as needed

1 tablespoon chopped garlic, plus 1 whole clove

½ teaspoon crushed red pepper

1 tablespoon finely chopped fresh sage

1 cup thinly sliced onions

½ cup roughly chopped celery

1 cup roughly chopped carrots

1 cup thinly sliced white of leeks

2 ounces (2 cups) dried porcini mushrooms, soaked in 3 cups warm water for ½ hour

1½ cups sliced cremini mushrooms

Salt

Freshly ground black pepper

6 ounces (2 cups) baby artichokes (or globe artichoke hearts and bottoms or frozen artichokes)

1 cup dry white wine

1 cup roughly chopped seeded red bell pepper

1½ pounds Swiss chard, washed, stems cut into 1-inch lengths, and leaves chopped and kept separate (6 cups total)

2 cups seeded diced fresh tomatoes

2 quarts vegetable stock or water

8 slices Tuscan bread

6 poached eggs (optional, see page 61, step 8)

½ cup grated Parmesan cheese

WINE SUGGESTION: *The garlic accents of this soup taste great with a red wine from Maremma, like Morellino I Perazzi.*

1 Coat the bottom of a stockpot with the olive oil. Add the chopped garlic, crushed red pepper, sage, onions, celery, carrots, and leeks and sauté over medium heat until the vegetables start to color, 10 to 15 minutes. Stir frequently to prevent sticking.

2 Scoop the porcini mushrooms out of the water without disturbing the sediment at the bottom and finely chop. Gently pour off 1 cup of the mushroom water and reserve. Add the chopped porcini and sliced cremini to the vegetable mixture. Season with salt and pepper and cook for 5 minutes.

3 If you are using baby artichokes, peel away the outer leaves until you reach the part where the leaves are mostly a creamy yellow. Cut the top inch off each artichoke and trim away the stem so that you are left with a golf ball-sized heart. Chop the hearts roughly and add to the pot. (For globe artichokes, remove the tough outer leaves and cut the artichokes into wedges. Remove the choke and the soft curly leaves above it. Chop and add to the pot.)

4 Add the wine and cook until reduced by half. Add the red bell pepper and Swiss chard stems and cook for 5 minutes.

5 Add the tomatoes, Swiss chard leaves, the 1 cup reserved mushroom water, and the vegetable stock or water. Simmer for 40 minutes.

6 In a toaster oven toast the slices of Tuscan bread. Brush them with olive oil, then rub each slice with the remaining whole garlic clove.

7 If using, place a poached egg in the bottom of each soup bowl and sprinkle with Parmesan. Ladle the soup over the egg, drizzle with olive oil, and sprinkle with freshly ground black pepper. Serve the garlic toast with the soup.

# MIRAO

## *Cristoforo Colombo's Chicken Soup*

According to Massimo Aalbereni, one of Italy's most important food historians, this soup was one of Cristoforo Colombo's favorites. As an old cookbook fan, I like to think Colombo found the recipe in the fifteenth-century volume, *Honest Pleasure and Good Health*, by Platina, one of the few cookbooks in existence at the time. Of course, we'll never know, but recipes like this one, which depended on slabs of bread to hold meat and vegetables, were staples in those pre-plate days. Once plates became popular, people retained the custom of using bread under their food. In this recipe, the croutons are as crucial to the dish as the chicken. Make the croutons big and crunchy. **SERVES 6 TO 8**

5 tablespoons extra virgin olive oil

1 cup thinly sliced onions

½ cup diagonally sliced carrot

¼ cup sliced garlic cloves

One 3- to 4-pound chicken, cut into 6 to 8 pieces

Salt

Freshly ground black pepper

½ cup brandy

6 whole cloves

3 bay leaves

½ cinnamon stick

1 whole nutmeg

2 sprigs rosemary

1 celery stalk, halved

¼ cup whole fresh Italian parsley leaves

16 slices day-old bread, toasted and rubbed with raw garlic

½ cup grated Parmesan cheese, for finishing

---

**WINE SUGGESTION:** *The first time I ever had Zinfandel was with this dish and it was a great combination. Unfortunately, we don't make Zif in Tuscany, so here I'd go with a Tuscan Syrah, like Cortona Il Bosco from Luigi D'Alessandro, which I like for its softness.*

---

1 Coat the bottom of a stockpot with 3 tablespoons of the olive oil. Add the onions, carrot, and garlic and sauté over medium until the vegetables start to soften but do not brown. Stir occasionally.

2 Season the chicken with salt and pepper and add it to the pot. Turn the chicken pieces over as they start to brown.

3 When the chicken and the vegetables have browned lightly, add the brandy and reduce by half.

4 Using a 6-inch square piece of cheesecloth, tie together the cloves, bay leaves, cinnamon stick, nutmeg, and rosemary.

5 Add water to cover the chicken, and season with salt and pepper. Add the herb bouquet and celery, bring to a simmer, and cook for 45 minutes to 1 hour.

6 Remove the chicken from the soup. Remove and discard the herb bouquet and the celery. Place the soup in the refrigerator to cool until the fat on top hardens. Remove the soup from the refrigerator and skim the fat off the surface. Reheat.

7 Meanwhile, preheat the broiler.

8 When the chicken is cool enough to handle, remove the skin, bones, and gristle. Shred the chicken into bite-sized pieces and return it to the soup. Taste for seasoning. Stir in the parsley leaves.

9 To serve, place a slice of garlic toast in each of 8 ovenproof soup bowls and ladle chicken and some of the soup over it. Top with a slice of toast. Drizzle the toasts with the remaining olive oil, sprinkle with grated Parmesan and pepper. Place the bowls under the broiler for 2 to 3 minutes, or until the cheese has melted and starts to brown.

# BRODO *di* POLLO

## *Chicken Stock*

This is great when you're under the weather. **MAKES 2 QUARTS**

3–4 pounds chicken legs

4 cups coarsely chopped celery

3 cups coarsely chopped carrots

1½ cups coarsely chopped onions

1 tablespoon salt

Combine all of the ingredients along with 4 quarts of water in a large pot and bring to a simmer. Cook, partially covered, for 1 hour. Add salt to taste and simmer, partially covered, for another hour. Strain into a large bowl, pressing on the chicken and vegetables to extract the liquid. Let cool.

# GNOCCHI
## *Basic Gnocchi*

When potatoes first arrived in Italy from the New World, a lot of people wouldn't eat them because they thought they caused leprosy. We obviously got over that and started eating them boiled and mashed into everything from pies to pasta. This is a basic gnocchi (Italian for dumpling) recipe; you can top them with anything you like, from pesto to wild boar sauce—or just a little tomato and parsley sautéed in butter and oil. If you have leftovers, which is likely, because the recipe makes a lot, just freeze them uncooked for another time. **SERVES 6 TO 8**

**FAST FRESH TOMATO SAUCE**

4 tablespoons extra virgin olive oil

2 garlic cloves

2½ cups seeded chopped plum tomatoes

2 tablespoons chopped fresh Italian parsley

1 tablespoon chopped fresh basil

4 tablespoons (½ stick) butter

Salt

Freshly ground black pepper

**WINE SUGGESTION:** *I like Morellino di Scansano I Perazzi, made by my friends Mario and Giuseppe, because it's easy to drink, especially with a simple dish like this.*

**THE GNOCCHI**

5 pounds Idaho potatoes, peeled and cut in 1¼-inch chunks (about 15 cups)

Salt

½ cup freshly grated Parmesan cheese

2 egg yolks and 1 whole egg

1 teaspoon grated nutmeg

⅓ cup ricotta cheese

1¾ cups flour, plus more for dusting

1 For the sauce: Coat the bottom of a large skillet with the olive oil. Smash the whole garlic cloves with the heel of your hand, add them to the skillet, and sauté over medium heat until they start to color and are very fragrant. Remove the cloves from the skillet and discard. Stir in the tomatoes, parsley, and basil. Swirl the skillet to incorporate all of the ingredients, season with salt and pepper to taste, and set aside.

2 For the gnocchi: Put the potatoes in a large pot and cover with cold water. Add a large pinch of salt. Bring the water to a boil and cook until the potatoes start to fall apart, 20 to 25 minutes. Drain and set the potatoes aside to cool.

*(continued)*

3  Force the potatoes through a ricer onto a baking sheet, then transfer them to a large bowl. Add the remaining ingredients and knead just until combined. Do not overwork the dough.

4  Dust a clean work surface with flour.

5  Knead the dough on the surface into a circle about 11 inches in diameter and 1 inch thick. Cut the dough into ½-inch-thick strips. Gently roll the strips with your palms into long, thin ropes, each about 12 to 18 inches long.

6  Slice the ropes into ½-inch chunks. Stamp each piece by holding a fork in one hand and gently rolling each gnocchi with the thumb of the other hand across the tines. Place the gnocchi on a tray dusted with flour so that they do not stick together. The gnocchi may be cooked immediately, refrigerated overnight, or stored frozen for up to 1 month. Freeze them on a tray in a single layer. After they are frozen, transfer them to freezer bags.

7  To cook, bring a large pot of salted water to a boil and add the gnocchi. They are done about 10 seconds after they rise to the surface. (If cooking frozen gnocchi, do not defrost them first. Place them in the boiling water right from the freezer. The cooking time may be a little longer.) So that they cook evenly, you will need to cook the gnocchi in batches.

8  Toss the gnocchi with the sauce and serve.

# STRANGOLAPRETI

## *Bread and Swiss Chard Gnocchi*

There's an Italian saying that's a little harsh: "Priests, pigs, and chickens, they're never satisfied," which goes back to the days when priests would drop by the homes of parishioners just in time for Sunday dinner. They got a reputation for eating so much that they couldn't get it all down. We call this variation on gnocchi *strangolapreti*, which literally translates as "priest chokers." In addition to tossing the gnocchi in butter and sage as suggested here, you can also serve them in a tomato sauce or *ragù*. SERVES 4 TO 6

16 cups day-old Tuscan bread, crusts removed and cut into 1-inch cubes

1 quart milk

4 cups tightly packed, stemmed Swiss chard leaves

2 eggs

½ cup grated Parmesan cheese, plus a little more for finishing

2 teaspoons finely chopped fresh thyme

Salt

Freshly ground black pepper

Pinch grated nutmeg

1 cup Bread Crumbs (page 27)

Flour

8 tablespoons (1 stick) butter

2 tablespoons finely chopped fresh sage

WINE SUGGESTION: *With these gnocchi, I'd definitely go with a white palate cleanser. Try Le Rime, a Pinot Grigio and Chardonnay blend.*

1 Soak the bread cubes in the milk for 30 minutes, or until all of the bread is soft. Squeeze out any excess milk and set aside.

2 Cook the Swiss chard in well-salted boiling water for 2 to 3 minutes. Drain the leaves and cool under cold running water. Using your hands, squeeze out as much water as possible. Coarsely chop the leaves.

3 In a food processor combine the softened bread, chopped Swiss chard, eggs, ½ cup Parmesan, thyme, salt and pepper to taste, nutmeg, and half of the bread crumbs. Puree to a smooth consistency. Transfer the mixture to a bowl. It should be very dry but hold its shape. If it's too moist, gradually add the remaining ½ cup bread crumbs.

*(continued)*

4 Coat your hands with flour and roll the mixture into ½-inch balls. Arrange the gnocchi on a well-floured baking sheet. The gnocchi may be cooked immediately, refrigerated overnight, or stored frozen for up to 1 month. Freeze them on a tray in a single layer. After they are frozen, transfer them to freezer bags.

5 To cook, bring a large pot of salted water to a boil and add the gnocchi. They are done about 10 seconds after they rise to the top. (If cooking frozen gnocchi, do not defrost them first. Place them in the boiling water right from the freezer. The cooking time may be a little longer.) So that they cook evenly, you will need to cook them in batches.

6 Preheat the broiler.

7 Melt the butter in a small saucepan over low heat. Add the sage and salt and pepper to taste.

8 Drain the gnocchi. Place them in a heatproof dish, toss with the sage butter, and sprinkle with Parmesan. Run the gnocchi under the broiler for a few minutes, until the cheese turns slightly brown and crispy.

# PAN *di* CINGHIALE

## *Wild Boar Gnocchi with Wild Boar Sauce*

The traditional way to make these gnocchi is with rabbit, but I started substituting boar because I like the stronger flavor. You can also experiment with pork or chicken. **SERVES** 8

### THE SAUCE

7 cups diced celery

1½ cups diced carrots

4 cups diced onions

6 whole garlic cloves

3 ounces pancetta, coarsely chopped (¾ cup)

3 juniper berries, crushed with the flat side of a knife

1 tablespoon finely chopped fresh rosemary

4 tablespoons finely chopped fresh sage

¼ cup extra virgin olive oil

### THE GNOCCHI

3 pounds boneless wild boar meat, cut into ¾-inch cubes (or pork shoulder or pork butt)

Salt

Freshly ground black pepper

1 cup dry red wine

2 cups canned whole tomatoes, with their juice, pureed (You can buy canned pureed tomatoes, but I think whole ones are less acidic and of better quality.)

3 bay leaves

Pinch grated nutmeg

1 cinnamon stick

Pinch ground cloves

10 cups day-old Tuscan bread, crusts removed and cut into 1-inch cubes

Bread Crumbs (optional, page 27)

½ cup grated Parmesan cheese, plus more for dusting

3 eggs

¼ cup finely chopped fresh Italian parsley

**WINE SUGGESTION:** *Wild boar is king in the region of Maremma, and the king of Maremma wines is the Super Tuscan, Ornellaia. It would be the perfect combination, but Ornellaia has become so expensive in the last few years let me suggest another good Cabernet blend from the area: Le Serre Nuove.*

*(continued)*

1  To make the sauce: In a food processor puree the celery, carrots, onions, garlic, pancetta, juniper berries, rosemary, and sage to a coarse paste.

2  Coat the bottom of a large skillet with the olive oil. Add the pureed vegetables and sauté over medium heat until the mixture starts to brown, 10 to 15 minutes. Stir frequently to prevent sticking.

3  Season the meat with salt and pepper to taste, add it to the pan, and brown on all sides.

4  Add the wine and cook until reduced by half. Add the tomatoes, bay leaves, nutmeg, cinnamon stick, cloves, and 3 cups water. Simmer for 1 hour. Add water a cup at a time, if needed, to prevent sauce from becoming too thick.

5  Remove one quarter of the sauce from the skillet and set aside. Add another cup of water, if needed, to the remaining sauce and continue to cook for 30 minutes. Adjust the seasonings and remove the bay leaves and cinnamon stick.

6  To make the gnocchi dough: In a large bowl combine the sauce, the day-old bread, ½ cup Parmesan, eggs, parsley, and salt and pepper to taste.

7  Transfer the mixture to a food processor in batches and blend until a smooth and homogeneous dough forms. (If you want firmer gnocchi, add bread crumbs, a spoonful at a time.) Roll the dough into ½-inch balls.

8  Preheat the broiler.

9  Bring a large pot of salted water to a boil and add the gnocchi. They are ready about 10 seconds after they float to the top. You will need to cook them in batches so they cook evenly. Drain.

10  Toss the gnocchi with the reserved sauce, and transfer to a large ovenproof dish. Dust with Parmesan and place under the broiler until the cheese becomes brown and crispy. Depending on the quantity of gnocchi, you will need to do this in batches. Serve.

# PASTA

## *Basic Pasta Dough*

Making pasta by hand takes patience and time. After a few times, you'll get it right.

**SERVES 6 TO 8, YIELD: 1¾ POUNDS**

> **4½ cups unbleached white flour**
>
> **4 large whole eggs, plus 4 large egg yolks**
>
> **2 teaspoons salt**

1  Mound the flour on a clean work surface and form a well in the center.

2  Add the eggs and the egg yolks to the well and scramble them with your fingers or with a fork.

3  Add in the olive oil, ½ cup water, and the salt.

4  Use one hand to mix in the eggs and the other to hold up the wall of the flour well from the outside. Gradually begin incorporating the flour from the inside wall of the well into the eggs.

5  When the eggs are no longer runny, push in the walls of the flour and work the mixture into a mound of soft crumbs. Gather the mass together and begin working it into a ball. (If it seems too dry, add another ¼ cup water, a tablespoon at a time.)

6  Once the dough has formed, knead it vigorously for 10 minutes, until it is elastic and smooth. Shape the dough into a flat oval, cover it with a kitchen towel, and let it rest for 1 hour. The dough is ready.

# RAVIOLI *di* PESCE
## *Seafood Ravioli*

Almost every region in Italy has its own variety of stuffed pasta: In Emilia Romagna, there are *tortellini* (little torts) and *cappelletti* (little hats); in Piedmonte, *agnolotti* (little lambs); and in Liguria, ravioli, which comes from the verb to wrap (*ravvolgere* in Italian). Since stuffed pastas require more work, they were typically made only on Sundays, holidays, or in honor of dinner guests. The traditional stuffed pasta from Lucca is *tordelli*, which have a meat filling, but I like filling them with seafood, which is traditional on the Tuscan coast. Making your own pasta dough can be challenging, but with experience, you'll get it right. SERVES 4 TO 6

**THE SAUCE**

3 tablespoons extra virgin olive oil

2 teaspoons chopped garlic

1½ cups seeded, chopped fresh plum tomatoes

2 tablespoons chopped fresh Italian parsley

2 tablespoons chopped fresh basil

2 tablespoons chopped fresh tarragon

Salt

Freshly ground black pepper

**THE RAVIOLI**

1 quart fish stock (or broth made from fish bouillon cubes)

1 pound boneless, skinless white fish fillets, such as bass, snapper, or sole

1 cup cubed, day-old white bread, crusts removed

½ cup whole milk

1 tablespoon chopped fresh Italian parsley

2 teaspoons minced garlic

Pinch crushed red pepper

1 tablespoon fresh lemon juice

2 whole eggs, plus eggwash of 2 eggs beaten with 2 tablespoons water

1½ pounds basic pasta dough (page 72)

Grated Parmesan cheese, for finishing

WINE SUGGESTION: *These ravioli are on the delicate side, so I'd pair them with a white, like Malvasia i Campetti, which is full, soft, and perfect with seafood.*

1 To make the sauce: Coat the bottom of a large skillet with the olive oil. Add the garlic to the skillet, and sauté over medium heat until it starts to color and is very fragrant. Stir in the tomatoes, 2 tablespoons of the parsley, 1 tablespoon of the basil, and the tarragon. Cook for 15 minutes. Season with salt and pepper to taste and set the sauce aside.

2 To make the ravioli: Bring the fish stock to a boil in a large saucepan. Reduce to a simmer, add the fish fillets, and cook for 5 to 7 minutes. Remove the fillets from the stock, transfer to a large bowl, and set aside.

3 In a bowl soak the bread cubes in the milk. You will need to submerge the bread with your hands to fully saturate it. Once the bread is wet, squeeze out excess milk. Add the bread to the fish.

4 Add the remaining 1 tablespoon parsley, the minced garlic, crushed red pepper, lemon juice, and salt and pepper to the fish. Transfer the mixture to a food processor and puree to a smooth paste. Taste for seasonings. Transfer the mixture to a large bowl and stir in the 2 whole eggs. Combine well, cover with plastic wrap, and refrigerate the filling.

5 Roll the prepared pasta dough to the number 5 or 6 setting on your pasta machine. Cut the sheets into manageable lengths, 12 to 15 inches long and 4 inches wide. Keep them covered with a damp cloth until ready to use.

6 Working with one sheet at a time, brush the pasta sheet with eggwash. Place 1 tablespoon of the prepared fish filling 1 inch from the left edge of the pasta sheet and 1 inch from the bottom horizontal edge. Place 1 tablespoon filling every 2 inches along the length of the pasta sheet.

7 Fold the top horizontal edge of the pasta over the mounds of filling to meet the bottom edge. Using your two index fingers, lightly press around each mound of the filling to remove any air bubbles and to seal the pasta.

8 Using a fluted pastry wheel or round cutter, cut the pasta around the filling, leaving only ½ inch between the edge of the pasta and the filling. Place the ravioli on a floured tray. The ravioli can be cooked immediately, refrigerated overnight, or stored frozen for up to a month. Freeze them on a tray in a single layer. After they are frozen, transfer them to freezer bags.

*(continued)*

9  To cook, bring a large pot of salted water to a boil and add the ravioli. Cook until just under *al dente*. Since it is fresh pasta, it won't take long. Drain, reserving 1 cup of the pasta cooking water.

10  Return the sauce to the heat and bring to a simmer. Add ½ cup of the cooking water and swirl it in to incorporate all of the ingredients. Add the ravioli and cook another 2 minutes. Make sure all the ravioli are coated with sauce. Stir in the remaining tablespoon of basil. Sprinkle with the Parmesan cheese and serve.

# RAVIOLI *con* CARCIOFI
## *Artichoke Ravioli*

My first *sous-chef* at Beppe, Gianmarco, has gone back to Italy to open his own restaurant, but when we were together we came up with new recipes all the time. Like these ravioli: We had boxes of extra artichokes and didn't know what to do with them, so we started experimenting with ways to soften, but not drown the artichoke flavor. You can make the pasta dough and/or filling the day ahead and assemble the ravioli when you're ready to cook. You can also freeze ravioli, but use them within a month. **SERVES 8 TO 10, ABOUT 60 RAVIOLI**

5 tablespoons extra virgin olive oil

5 teaspoons minced garlic

2½ cups chopped fresh tomatoes

2 tablespoons chopped fresh basil

2 tablespoons finely chopped fresh marjoram

2 tablespoons finely chopped fresh Italian parsley

Pinch crushed red pepper

Salt

Freshly ground black pepper

2 lemons

8 medium artichokes, or 12 small artichokes

½ cup dry white wine

2 cups vegetable stock or water

½ cup ricotta or mascarpone cheese

⅓ cup grated Parmesan cheese, plus more for serving

1½ pounds basic Pasta Dough (page 73)

Eggwash of 2 eggs beaten with 2 tablespoons water

**WINE SUGGESTION:** *A Pinot Grigio would go well with the artichokes in this dish. Try San Angelo, a Pinot Grigio that is made right in Tuscany.*

1  Coat the bottom of a large skillet with 3 tablespoons of the olive oil. Add 2 teaspoons garlic to the skillet with the tomatoes, and cook over medium heat for 15 minutes.

2  Stir in 1 tablespoon of the basil, 1 tablespoon of the marjoram, 1 tablespoon of the parsley, and the crushed red pepper. Season with salt and pepper to taste and transfer sauce to a bowl. Set aside.

*(continued)*

3  Fill a large bowl with water and squeeze the juice of both lemons into it. Trim the tough outer leaves from the artichokes, cut them into quarters, and cut out the hairy chokes from the centers. Put the trimmed artichoke immediately in the bowl of acidulated water. Set aside.

4  Wipe the skillet clean and coat the bottom with the remaining 2 tablespoons of olive oil. Add the remaining garlic, remaining 1 tablespoon marjoram, remaining 1 tablespoon parsley, and crushed red pepper to taste and sauté over medium heat until the garlic begins to color, 2 to 3 minutes.

5  Drain the artichokes, add them to the skillet, and cook for 3 to 4 minutes.

6  Add the wine, vegetable stock or water, and salt and pepper. Cook over high heat for 15 minutes, or until the bottoms of the artichokes are tender when tested with a fork. Remove the pan from the heat and let the artichokes cool in their cooking liquid.

7  Drain the artichokes, garlic, and herbs and place them in the bowl of a food processor. Add the ricotta or mascarpone, Parmesan, and salt and pepper to taste and puree. Set the filling aside.

8  Roll the prepared pasta dough to the number 5 or 6 setting on your pasta machine. Cut the sheets into manageable lengths, 12 to 15 inches long and 4 inches wide. Keep them covered with a damp cloth until ready to use.

9  Working with one sheet at a time, brush the pasta with eggwash. Place 1 tablespoon of the prepared filling 1 inch from the left edge and 1 inch from the lower horizontal edge. Place 1 tablespoon filling every two inches along the length of the pasta sheet.

10 Fold the top horizontal edge of the pasta over the mounds of filling to meet the bottom edge. Using your two index fingers, lightly press around each mound of filling to remove any air bubbles and to seal the pasta.

11 Using a fluted pastry wheel or round cutter, cut the pastry around the filling, leaving only ½ inch between the edge of the pasta and the filling. Place the ravioli on a floured tray and reserve. The ravioli can be used immediately, refrigerated overnight, or stored frozen for up to 1 month. Freeze them on a tray in a single layer. After they are frozen, transfer them to freezer bags.

12 To cook, bring a large pot of salted water to a boil and add the ravioli. Cook until just under *al dente*. Since it is fresh pasta, it won't take long, 2 to 3 minutes, depending on the thickness of the dough. Drain, reserving 1 cup of the pasta cooking water.

13 Return the sauce to the stove and bring to a simmer. Add ½ cup of the reserved cooking water and swirl it in the pan. Add the ravioli and cook another 2 minutes, adding more water if necessary. Stir in the remaining tablespoon of basil. Sprinkle with Parmesan and serve.

# RAVIOLI *di* RICOTTA *e* SPINACI

## *Spinach and Ricotta Ravioli*

In the seventeenth century, Neapolitans were called *mangiafoglie*, or leaf-eaters, because they ate so much lasagna. The Ligurians converted those noodles into ravioli, similar to the stuffed pasta we eat today. I like this recipe because it's all about greens, one of the Ligurians' favorite foods. Even the famous nineteenth-century gourmet Artusi noted that real ravioli should be filled with greens or greens and cheese since that's the way they do it in Liguria—but it's a favorite preparation in Tuscany, too. **SERVES 8 TO 10, ABOUT 60 RAVIOLI**

Fast Fresh Tomato Sauce (page 67)

**THE RAVIOLI**

1 pound spinach, stems removed

1½ cups ricotta cheese

2 whole eggs, plus eggwash of 2 eggs beaten with 2 tablespoons water

1 cup grated Parmesan cheese

Pinch grated nutmeg

1½ pounds basic Pasta Dough (page 73)

**WINE SUGGESTION:** *We've been eating this dish in Tuscany for centuries, but to mix it up, I'd go with a new wine, like Pinot Noir from Pancrazi.*

1 For the ravioli: Cook the spinach in a large pot of well-salted boiling water for 1 to 2 minutes, or until wilted. Drain and cool under cold running water. Using your hands, squeeze out as much water as possible from the spinach. Finely chop.

2 In a large bowl combine the chopped spinach, ricotta, the 2 whole eggs, and Parmesan. Season with nutmeg and salt and pepper. Set aside.

3 Roll the prepared pasta dough to the number 5 or 6 setting on your pasta machine. Cut the sheets into manageable lengths, 12 to 15 inches long by 4 inches wide. Keep them covered with a damp cloth until ready to use. The pasta sheets will keep for a day in the refrigerator.

4  Flour your work surface lightly. Working with one sheet at a time, brush the pasta with eggwash. Place 1 tablespoon of the prepared spinach filling 1 inch from the left edge of the pasta sheet and 1 inch up from the bottom horizontal edge. Place 1 tablespoon of filling every 2 inches along the length of the pasta sheet.

5  Fold the top horizontal edge of the pasta down over the mounds of filling to meet the bottom edge. Using your two index fingers, lightly press around each mound of the filling to remove any air bubbles and to seal the pasta.

6  Using a fluted pastry wheel or round cutter, cut the pasta around the filling, leaving only ½ inch between the edge of the pasta and the filling. Place the ravioli on a floured tray and reserve. The ravioli can be cooked immediately, refrigerated overnight, or stored frozen for up to 1 month. Freeze them on a tray in a single layer. After they are frozen, transfer them to freezer bags.

7  To cook, bring a large pot of salted water to a boil and add the ravioli. Cook until just under *al dente*. Since it is fresh pasta, it won't take long, 2 to 3 minutes, depending on the thickness of the dough. You will need to cook the ravioli in batches so they cook evenly. Drain, reserving 1 cup of the pasta cooking water.

8  Return the sauce to the stove and bring it to a simmer. Add ½ cup of the cooking water and swirl it in to incorporate all of the ingredients. Add the ravioli and cook another 2 minutes, adding more water if necessary.

# LASAGNE COLL'OCCHI

## *Lasagna with Black-eyed Peas*

Black-eyed pea lasagna might sound like fusion cuisine gone awry, but it is authentically Italian. Lasagna was among the first pastas invented: It was called *lagana* by the Romans who ate the noodles pan-fried, not boiled. Until the discovery of America, black-eyed peas were the only bean we had in Italy. Some say Catherine de' Medici invented this dish, but even if she didn't, we know it was a staple on Florentine menus of her day and that the recipe inspired the famous *pasta e fagioli* soup. While Americans think of lasagna as a baked dish, with layers of pasta, sauce, vegetables, and cheese, in Italy it's not uncommon to treat lasagna like other noodles and simply toss them with sauce. **SERVES 4 TO 6**

1 cup dried black-eyed peas

2 celery stalks, cut in thirds, plus ½ cup coarsely chopped celery

1 carrot, cut in half, plus ½ cup coarsely chopped carrots

1 onion, quartered, plus 1 cup coarsely chopped onions

Salt

1 tablespoon roughly chopped garlic

1 teaspoon crushed red pepper

1 teaspoon finely chopped fresh sage

1 teaspoon finely chopped fresh rosemary

6 anchovy fillets (I prefer the taste of salted anchovies, but they need to be soaked in white wine or water for a few hours or overnight before using.)

3 tablespoons extra virgin olive oil, plus more for drizzling

½ cup dry white wine

2 tablespoons fresh Italian parsley

½ cup canned whole tomatoes, with their juice, pureed (You can use canned pureed tomatoes, but I think the whole ones are less acidic and of higher quality.)

1 pound dried lasagna, broken into pieces

¼ cup grated Parmesan cheese, or more to taste, for serving

Freshly ground black pepper

---

**WINE SUGGESTION:** *I like Remole, a blend of Sangiovese and Cabernet Sauvignon grapes. It's made by Frescobaldi, one of Italy's oldest wineries, with a family tree that dates back to the 1300s.*

---

1 Rinse the black-eyed peas and pick them over for stones, debris, and broken peas. Place the peas in a large pot with 4 quarts cold water, the cut celery stalks, the halved carrot, and the quartered onion. Bring to a boil and simmer for 1½ hours. Five minutes before removing them from the heat, add salt to taste. The beans are done when they are creamy on the inside. Drain and set aside. (To save time, you can use 2 cups frozen black-eyed peas, following the instructions on the package, or 2 cups canned black-eyed peas, rinsed well.)

2 In a food processor puree the chopped celery, carrots, and onions with the garlic, crushed red pepper, sage, rosemary, and anchovies to a coarse paste.

3 Coat the bottom of a large skillet with the 3 tablespoons olive oil. Add the pureed vegetable mixture and sauté over medium heat for 12 to 15 minutes until the vegetables start to soften and brown.

4 Add the wine and cook until reduced by half.

5 Add the parsley and tomatoes with the beans and 2 cups water. Simmer the mixture over medium heat for 20 to 25 minutes, stirring occasionally to prevent sticking and burning. Add more water if needed.

6 While the bean mixture is simmering, bring a large pot of salted water to a boil. Add the lasagna and cook until it is *al dente*. Drain. Add a little olive oil to keep the noodles from sticking. Set aside.

7 When the bean sauce has finished simmering, stir in the lasagna and simmer for 3 to 4 minutes. Transfer the lasagna to a serving bowl and top with the Parmesan, a drizzle of olive oil, and a sprinkling of black pepper.

# PASTICCIO CO'FUNGHI
## *Mushroom Lasagna*

*Pasticcio* translates as "what a mess!" and while this version is a lot less messy than the similarly named dish Pasticcio alla Fiorentina, (page 86), it still looks like a jumble on the plate. I used to eat this growing up. It is a typical dish from Garfagnana, the area my mother comes from, and just one mouthful brings back my summers as a teenager. I'd drive around with my dad, looking for cases of the best mushrooms in Tuscany, which my mom would transform into the tastiest *pasticcio* ever. Try splitting up the work by making the Béchamel and mushroom sauce a day ahead. **SERVES 4 TO 6**

½ ounce (½ cup) dried porcini mushrooms

3–4 tablespoons extra virgin olive oil

1 tablespoon minced garlic

2 tablespoons finely chopped fresh Italian parsley

1½ pounds fresh mixed mushrooms, sliced (preferably a mixture of shiitake, oyster, or cremini)

Salt

Freshly ground black pepper

½ cup dry white wine

1 pound dried lasagna

2 egg yolks

2 cups Béchamel Sauce (page 86)

¼ cup grated Parmesan cheese

**WINE SUGGESTION:** *Hands down, drink Lucente, a new wine that's a collaboration between the Frescobaldi and Robert Mondavi wineries. Mostly Sangiovese and Merlot grapes with a little Cabernet Sauvignon, Lucente has the body and spice to compliment this lasagna.*

1  Soak the porcini in 1 quart warm water for ½ hour. Using your hand, scoop the porcini out of the water, trying not to disturb the sediment on the bottom. Coarsely chop the porcini and set aside. Gently pour off 2⅓ cups of the soaking water into another container and reserve. Discard the remaining soaking water.

2  Preheat the oven to 400° F.

3  Coat the bottom of a large skillet with 3 tablespoons olive oil. Add the garlic and parsley and sauté over medium heat until the garlic just begins to color.

4 Add the chopped porcini and the fresh mushrooms and sauté until very soft, 5 to 7 minutes. Season with salt and pepper to taste.

5 Add the reserved porcini water and wine and cook until the liquid has almost reduced completely, but don't let the pan go dry. Turn off the heat and set aside.

6 Bring a large pot of salted water to a boil. Add the lasagna and cook until it is just under *al dente*. Drain, and cool under cold running water for 2 to 3 minutes. Add a little olive oil to keep the noodles from sticking. Set aside.

7 Whisk the egg yolks into the Béchamel sauce and combine with the sautéed mushroom mixture.

8 Grease a 13- by 9-inch ovenproof dish with butter or olive oil. Dust with some of the Parmesan. Line the bottom of the dish with one layer of the lasagna noodles, spoon a thick layer of the mushroom filling mixture over the noodles, and sprinkle with Parmesan. Top with a layer of noodles and cover with a thin layer of filling. Sprinkle with Parmesan. Bake for 35 to 40 minutes. When done, the top should look slightly brown and crispy. Remove the lasagna from the oven and allow it to sit for 15 to 20 minutes before serving.

# PASTICCIO *alla* FIORENTINA
## *Renaissance Pasta Timbale*

This lampshade-sized dish is more than a meal, it's a multiday production. (You might even remember it as the star of the banquet scene in the movie *Big Night*.) In the Renaissance, this kind of overstuffed dish was the centerpiece of aristocratic dining tables and Medici daughters' weddings. Cooks filled it with the showiest ingredients they could find, from goose to trout to candied orange peel and hare. My version is a little more streamlined for modern tastes, but still takes planning to pull off. My suggestion is to pace yourself and make at least the Béchamel sauce, *ragù*, and pastry the day before. Just so you know, there will be quite a bit of leftover *ragù*: I strongly believe that if you're going to the trouble of making this labor-intensive sauce, you want extra. Put it in an airtight container and freeze it. It will keep for up to six months. Or, if you're not like me, halve the *ragù* ingredients and you'll have the right amount for the timbale.

By the way, if you're wondering why timbale is translated as *pasticcio* and not *timballo*, it's because the words are really interchangeable all over Italy. In this case, I use the word timbale because that's how I found it in a Florentine manuscript. **SERVES** 8

**WINE SUGGESTION:** *With such a rich dish, I like to serve a big wine, like Pietradonice, which is mostly Cabernet Sauvignon. A simpler Rosso di Montalcino would be good, too.*

## BÉCHAMEL SAUCE
**MAKES** 4 **CUPS**

| | |
|---|---|
| 8 tablespoons (1 stick) butter | Pinch grated nutmeg |
| ½ cup flour | Salt |
| 1 quart whole milk | Freshly ground black pepper |

Melt the butter in a heavy saucepan. Add the flour and cook over low heat, stirring, for 4 to 5 minutes. Gradually whisk in the milk. Continue whisking to remove any lumps and to prevent the sauce from sticking to the bottom of the pan. Bring the sauce to a boil, continually whisking. Once the sauce has boiled, remove the pan from the heat and season with salt and pepper and nutmeg. Let cool and refrigerate until ready to use. The sauce will keep for 2 days.

# RAGÙ

MAKES 4 CUPS

½ cup coarsely chopped carrots

1½ cups coarsely chopped celery

1 cup coarsely chopped red onions

2 garlic cloves, peeled

2 tablespoons fresh rosemary leaves

½ cup chopped fresh Italian parsley (leaves and stems)

¼ cup extra virgin olive oil

4 ounces finely chopped pancetta (1 cup)

½ pound ground beef

¾ pound ground pork (You can use all beef or all pork or any combination to make 1¼ pounds total ground meat.)

½ cup dry red wine

½ cup tomato paste

1 cup canned whole tomatoes, with their juice, pureed (You can use canned pureed tomatoes, but I think the whole ones are less acidic and of better quality.)

Salt

Freshly ground black pepper

Pinch crushed red pepper

1 teaspoon Tuscan Spice (see Sources on page 221), or *garam masala*, or mix together equal parts of ground allspice, cinnamon, nutmeg, and cloves

1  In a food processor puree the carrots, celery, red onions, garlic, rosemary, and parsley to a coarse paste.

2  Coat the bottom of a large pot with the olive oil. Add the vegetable puree and sauté over medium-high until the mixture starts to color and turns aromatic, 10 to 15 minutes. Stir frequently to prevent sticking.

3  Add the pancetta and ground meats. Cook, stirring occasionally, until brown, about 10 minutes.

4  Add the wine. Stir and cook until it is completely evaporated, 5 to 10 minutes. Add the tomato paste, pureed tomatoes and 6 cups cold water. Stir to combine.

*(continued)*

5 Bring the sauce to a boil, reduce the heat, cover the pot, and simmer for 1 hour, stirring frequently to make sure the bottom isn't burning. If the sauce is reducing too quickly, add more water.

6 Add salt and pepper, crushed red pepper, and the Tuscan Spice. Cover and simmer for another hour, stirring frequently. Adjust the seasonings. Cool and refrigerate until ready to use. The sauce will keep for up to 1 week in the refrigerator or 6 months in the freezer. Cool properly in a shallow dish before storing in the refrigerator or freezer.

### PASTRY DOUGH

4 cups flour

2 tablespoons sugar

2 teaspoons salt

1 teaspoon freshly ground black pepper

16 tablespoons (2 sticks) butter, cut into small pieces

4 eggs

1 In a food processor combine the flour, sugar, salt, and pepper. Add the butter and pulse until the mixture resembles cornmeal. Add the eggs and pulse another 2 to 3 times. Add 1 to 2 tablespoons water if the mixture is very dry.

2 Turn the contents of the bowl of the food processor out onto a clean work surface and gather the dough together with your hands. Form into a disk, wrap in plastic wrap, and refrigerate for at least 30 minutes or no longer than 24 hours.

4 ounces (4 cups) dried porcini mushrooms, sliced (If porcini are not available, shiitake or oyster mushrooms can be substituted.)

7 tablespoons extra virgin olive oil

1½ pounds Tuscan Meat Loaf mixture, rolled into ½-inch balls (page 168)

4 cups Ragù (page 87)

4 cups Béchamel Sauce (page 86)

Salt

½ pound rigatoni or penne

1 teaspoon minced garlic

2 tablespoons chopped anchovy fillets (about 8–10) in oil (I prefer the taste of salted anchovies, but they need to be soaked in white wine or water for a few hours or overnight before using.)

2 tablespoons finely chopped fresh Italian parsley

Freshly ground black pepper

Pastry Dough (page 88)

2 cups Sautéed Spinach (page 186)

6 eggs, hard-boiled, peeled, and sliced thin

Grated Parmesan cheese

Eggwash: 1 egg beaten with 1 tablespoon water

1 Soak the porcini in warm water for a ½ hour.

2 Coat the bottom of a large skillet with ¼ cup of the olive oil and heat over medium heat. Add the meatballs and brown on all sides. Set aside.

3 In another large skillet combine the *ragù* and Béchamel sauce. Cook over medium heat for 10 minutes, stirring frequently. Remove from the heat and let cool.

4 Bring a large pot of salted water to a boil. Add the rigatoni and cook until just under *al dente*. Drain. Add to the Béchamel/*ragù* sauce and toss well. Set aside.

5 Coat the bottom of another large skillet with the remaining 3 tablespoons olive oil. Add the garlic, anchovies, and parsley and sauté over medium heat until the garlic just begins to color.

*(continued)*

6 Using your hand, scoop the porcini out of the water, trying not to disturb the sediment on the bottom. Discard the water. Add the porcini to the skillet and sauté until very soft, 6 to 7 minutes. Season with salt and pepper. Add to the pasta/*ragù* mixture. Add the browned meatballs.

7 Preheat the oven to 350° F. Butter and flour an 11-inch springform pan.

8 Divide the dough into 2 unequal pieces; the larger should be twice as big as the smaller.

9 On a well-floured surface roll the larger piece of dough into a large round about ⅛ inch thick and 15 inches in diameter. Fit into the prepared springform pan. There should be a long overhang of dough. Roll out the remaining dough into a round ¼ inch thick and about 11 inches in diameter. Set aside.

10 Place half of the pasta/*ragù*/mushroom mixture in the springform pan.

11 Add one layer each of spinach and hard-boiled egg slices.

12 Top with the remaining pasta mixture and sprinkle with grated Parmesan cheese.

13 Place the reserved dough on top of the filling. Using scissors or a sharp knife, trim the edges of the top dough to meet the edge of the pan. Brush with the prepared eggwash. Fold the overhanging dough of the bottom crust up over the top dough. Brush the edges with eggwash. Cut several holes in the top crust to allow steam to escape. Bake for 1 hour.

14 When done, the crust should be very firm, shiny, and golden brown. Let the timbale rest for at least 30 minutes. Loosen the timbale from the pan by running a knife around the inside edge of the pan. Remove the sides of the pan, transfer the timbale to a plate, slice, and serve.

# GEMELLI *con* MELANZANE

## *Pasta Norma*

When tomatoes first made their way to Sicily in the 1830s, locals used them to update traditional dishes like *caponata* (a Sicilian salad of eggplant, onions, and capers) and to give birth to some new ones, like *pasta alla norma*, which I translate as pasta the normal way, since it is so popular. Joking aside, the name comes from the opera, *Norma*, which was written by the Sicilian composer Vincenzo Bellini. This is another Sicilian dish, but since my mother made it for me when I was growing up, I consider it an honorary Tuscan one!

SERVES 4 TO 6

Salt

6 cups peeled diced eggplant

3 cups diced fresh tomatoes (no need to peel or seed)

1 cup extra virgin olive oil

Freshly ground black pepper

5 torn fresh basil leaves, plus ¼ cup roughly chopped fresh basil leaves

½ cup flour

4–5 cups canola or peanut oil for frying

2 tablespoons minced garlic

1 teaspoon crushed red pepper

1 teaspoon dried oregano

1 pound gemelli, or penne or other short pasta

2 tablespoons chopped fresh Italian parsley

1 cup cubed fresh mozzarella

3 tablespoons grated Parmesan cheese

---

WINE SUGGESTION: *Try a Sicilian rosé, like Rose di Regaleali or a Tuscan Rosato from Castello d'Ama.*

---

1 Salt the eggplant liberally and put in colander to drain for 1 hour.

2 Toss the tomatoes with ½ cup of the olive oil, salt and pepper to taste, and the 5 torn basil leaves. Set aside.

3 Dry the eggplant with paper towels and in a bowl toss with the flour.

4 Pour enough canola or peanut oil into a large skillet to come halfway up the sides of the pan. Heat to 375° F. on a candy thermometer. Add the eggplant and fry until golden brown. Remove with a slotted spoon and drain well on paper towels. Set aside.

*(continued)*

5 Discard the oil and wipe the skillet clean with a paper towel. Coat the bottom of the skillet with ¼ cup of the remaining olive oil. Add the garlic and crushed red pepper and sauté until the garlic begins to color.

6 Add the tomatoes, 1 tablespoon of the chopped basil, and the oregano and cook for 3 to 4 minutes, stirring frequently. Add the fried eggplant and season with a pinch of salt.

7 Bring a large pot of salted water to a boil and add the gemelli or penne. Cook until the pasta is just under *al dente*. Drain, reserving 1 cup of the cooking water.

8 Add the pasta to the sauce with ½ cup of the reserved cooking water. Cook for 2 to 3 minutes, adding more of the pasta water if the mixture is dry. Stir in the remaining basil, the parsley, mozzarella, and Parmesan.

9 When the mozzarella starts to melt, add 3 tablespoons of the remaining olive oil and stir until the cheese melts into the sauce. Serve immediately.

# PASTA *alla* CHECCA
## *Fusilli with Tomatoes and Fresh Mozzarella*

This, to me, is the ultimate summer pasta—raw tomatoes, basil, and garlic—and it is served all over Italy when tomatoes and basil are at their best. Though the dish didn't originate in Tuscany, we've been eating it for as long as we've had mozzarella. Insist on the highest quality tomatoes and cheese—otherwise, what's the point? If your tomatoes aren't as flavorful as they could be, one trick is to prepare the sauce a few hours before serving and let it steep so that the oil absorbs some of the flavor of the garlic. **SERVES 4 TO 6**

1 teaspoon chopped garlic

8–9 cups chopped ripe tomatoes (no need to peel or seed)

15 fresh basil leaves, in chiffonade

1 teaspoon crushed red pepper

2 teaspoons finely chopped fresh oregano

¼ cup extra virgin olive oil

Salt

Freshly ground black pepper

1 pound fusilli or penne

One 1¼- to 1½-pound ball fresh mozzarella, diced

4 tablespoons grated Parmesan cheese for finishing

**WINE SUGGESTION:** *Since this is a summer dish, best when tomatoes are at their height, I like a younger red served slightly chilled. One choice would be Col di Sasso, which translated means stony hill. It's made from Cabernet and Sangiovese grapes.*

1  In a large bowl combine the garlic, tomatoes, basil, red pepper, oregano, olive oil, and salt and pepper to taste. (If you have time, make the sauce 2 hours in advance to let the sauce marinate.)

2  Bring a large pot of salted water to a boil and add the pasta. Cook until *al dente*. Drain, transfer the pasta to a large bowl, and toss with the tomato sauce. Add the mozzarella, stirring so that the cheese starts to melt. Sprinkle with the Parmesan and serve immediately.

# CRESTE *con* GAMBERI *e* CANELLINI

## *Ruffled Pasta with Shrimp and Beans*

The classic Italian combination of shrimp and beans is here combined with another classic, pasta. Look for boxes of commercial ruffled pasta, but you can also substitute any short pasta you like. If you can find *cicerchie* (see Sources on page 221), an ancient bean that comes from central Italy, substitute those for the cannellini. *Cicerchie* have a unique, nutty flavor that will dress up the dish. **SERVES 4 TO 6**

6 whole garlic cloves, plus 2 teaspoons minced garlic

½ cup extra virgin olive oil

Salt

1 pound bow ties or other short ruffled pasta

5 whole fresh sage leaves

2 tablespoons chopped anchovies (about 8–10) in oil (I prefer the taste of salted anchovies, but they need to be soaked in white wine or water for a few hours or overnight before using.)

½ teaspoon crushed red pepper

1 cup dry white wine

6 cups cooked cannellini beans, plus 2 cups bean cooking water (page 187)

2 tablespoons chopped fresh Italian parsley

½ pound shelled shrimp, deveined and cut into thirds

¼ cup grated Parmesan cheese

---

**WINE SUGGESTION:** *I'd go with a full-bodied white here—a Chardonnay blend, like Fontanelle.*

---

1  Preheat the oven to 375° F.

2  Toss the 6 garlic cloves with 1 tablespoon of the olive oil and salt to taste. Bake on a baking sheet, shaking occasionally, about 30 minutes, or until soft. Reserve.

3  Bring a large pot of well-salted water to a boil. Add the pasta and cook until just under *al dente*. Drain, reserving 1 cup of the cooking water. Set aside.

4  Coat the bottom of a pan large enough to hold all the ingredients with ¼ cup of the remaining olive oil. Add the roasted garlic, sage leaves, anchovies, and half of the crushed red pepper and sauté over medium heat until the anchovies have started to break apart and dissolve, 5 to 7 minutes.

5  Add the wine and reduce by half.

6  Add the beans and the bean cooking water and simmer for 5 to 10 minutes.

7  Puree half of the bean mixture in a food processor to a smooth paste. Transfer to a bowl. Using the back of a fork or a potato masher, slightly crush the remaining beans and add them to the pureed bean mixture. Set aside.

8  Wipe the pan clean and coat it with the remaining 3 tablespoons olive oil. Add the minced garlic, the remaining crushed red pepper, and parsley and sauté over medium heat until the garlic begins to color, about 5 minutes.

9  Add the shrimp and sauté until they begin to turn pink, 1 to 2 minutes. Add the bean mixture and the cooked pasta. Toss to combine, adding some of the reserved pasta water if the mixture seems very thick. Cook for 2 to 3 minutes for the pasta to absorb some of the sauce. Toss with the grated Parmesan cheese and serve.

# MACCHERONCINI DEL BENGODI

## *Orecchiette with Parmesan and Black Pepper in Chicken Broth*

The medieval writer Giovanni Boccaccio is one of my heroes, just for inspiring this dish. He sets the scene for it in the *Decameron*, a novella that unfolds in the fictional town of Bengodi, which is built from a mountain of Parmesan cheese. At certain times of the year, knots of pasta materialize just like that, roll down a mountain made of Parmesan, and are harvested by the locals, who cook them in capon broth. I read that passage and thought, I have to make this dish. I shape the pasta like over-sized *orecchiette* and use chicken broth instead of capon broth. You'll need to double the recipe for chicken broth. SERVES 4 TO 6

2½ cups semolina flour (available in specialty stores), plus additional for dusting; all purpose flour will also work

Salt

1 tablespoon freshly ground black pepper

2 eggs

5 tablespoons extra virgin olive oil

4 quarts Chicken Broth (page 66) (or good-quality canned broth)

½ cup grated Parmesan cheese

2 tablespoons finely chopped fresh Italian parsley

WINE SUGGESTION: *This dish is spicy but delicate and needs a wine that is soft but can stand up to the pepper. My choice would be a big-style Merlot from Tuscany, like Lamaione from Castelgiocondo.*

1 Place the flour, salt and a pinch of black pepper in the bowl of an electric mixer or food processor. Mix on low for 1 minute. Add the eggs and 2 tablespoons of the olive oil. Increase the speed to medium and blend for 2½ to 3 minutes.

2 When the eggs and oil have been incorporated, add ½ cup water. The dough will form in about 2 minutes.

3 Remove the dough from the bowl and place on a flat clean surface dusted with flour. Knead for 3 minutes. The dough should be dry and fairly firm. Wrap the dough in plastic wrap and let rest in the refrigerator for at least 1 hour or up to 24 hours.

4  To cut the dough: Divide the dough in 6 pieces. Roll each piece into a rope about ½ inch thick. Slice each rope into thin disks, about ⅛ inch thick. In the center of each disk make a thumbprint. Place the rounds on a large tray, dust the pasta with semolina flour, and refrigerate until ready to use. The pasta will keep for a day in the refrigerator or up to a month in the freezer

5  To cook, bring the chicken broth to a boil in a large pot, add the pasta, and cook until just under *al dente*, stirring occasionally. Drain the pasta, reserving the broth. In a bowl mix the pasta with a bit of olive oil to keep them from sticking together. Set aside.

6  In a large skillet combine 1½ cups chicken broth and the remaining 3 tablespoons olive oil and bring to a boil. Add the pasta and cook 3 minutes. Add ¼ cup of the Parmesan, the parsley, and the tablespoon of black pepper. Stir, and cook 30 seconds to 1 minute. Divide among bowls, sprinkle with the remaining Parmesan, and serve.

# PINCI *con* SALSA
## *"Pinched" Pasta and Sauce*

This is a recipe for homemade fresh pasta that started off as a variation on the spaghetti noodle. A century ago, the noodle was a mainstay in the diet of peasants who dressed it with a little bit of olive oil or just salt and chopped onions or garlic. As life became easier, the noodles themselves got richer, with eggs and Parmesan added. And people began incorporating more ingredients into the sauce, too, like mushrooms or tomatoes. Eventually the sauce evolved into a full-bodied *ragù*. Of all the versions of this dish, I like the one from Montalcino best, where the noodles are made with coarse hand-milled flour and cheese.

Making this pasta is not easy; it can be hard to get the right quality noodles, even after many tries. In fact, I recommend keeping a box of spaghetti on hand as a backup. If you want your dinner to be really authentic, do it Italian family style, and teach the kids how to roll the strands. **SERVES** 6

**THE SAUCE**

⅓ cup extra virgin olive oil

3 tablespoons chopped garlic

¼ cup chopped anchovies (about 20) in oil (I prefer the taste of salted anchovies, but they need to be soaked in white wine or water for a few hours or overnight before using.)

1 teaspoon crushed red pepper

1 cup finely chopped black Italian olives

¼ cup chopped fresh Italian parsley

¾ cup finely chopped toasted walnuts

1 cup dry red wine

4 cups canned whole tomatoes, with their juices, pureed (You can also use canned pureed tomatoes, but I think the quality of whole tomatoes is better.)

¼ cup capers in brine, rinsed and finely chopped (I prefer capers packed in salt because they have more flavor, but you need to rinse and soak them in water for at least 6 hours before using.)

¼ cup shredded fresh basil

**WINE SUGGESTION:** Pinci *is a typical dish in and around Siena and Montalcino, so I'd go with one of the really good local wines, Brunello di Montalcino Silvio Nardi, or a simpler Rosso di Montalcino.*

| | |
|---|---|
| 3¾ cups all-purpose flour | Salt |
| 2 tablespoons grated Parmesan cheese, plus more for finishing | 3 eggs |
| | 2 tablespoons extra virgin olive oil |

1 To make the sauce: Coat the bottom of a large skillet with the olive oil. Add the garlic, anchovies, and crushed red pepper and sauté over medium heat until the garlic starts to color, about 5 minutes. Add the olives and parsley and cook for 2 to 3 minutes. Stir in the walnuts.

2 Add the wine and cook until reduced by half.

3 Add the tomatoes, capers, and basil and simmer for 20 to 30 minutes. Set the sauce aside.

4 To make the *pinci*: Combine the flour, the 2 tablespoons Parmesan, and 1 tablespoon salt in the bowl of a standing mixer. With the dough hook attachment and the machine on medium speed, add the eggs, one at a time, beating after each addition. Slowly drizzle in the olive oil. Gradually add ½ cup water, adding up to ¼ cup additional water if necessary to make a pliable dough. (The entire ¾ cup water may not be necessary.) Work the dough in the mixer until it has a smooth homogeneous consistency and firm texture.

5 Remove dough from the bowl and cut it into quarters. Run each piece of dough through a pasta machine set on the largest setting. (You may need to do this several times, dusting generously with flour.) If the dough seems to pucker and dimple, dust with flour, fold it in half, and run it through the machine several more times. The result should be long, smooth, thick sheets of pasta. Cut each sheet into 8–10 inch lengths. Using a straight-edged pastry wheel or pizza cutter, cut each sheet of pasta lengthwise into ¼-inch strips.

*(continued)*

6  Working with one strip at a time on the table, use your fingers to mold or "pinch" each pasta strip into a thin rope. Then, between the palms of your hands, roll the pasta into a rope. The pinching will aid in the rolling. (The end result will look like very fat strands of spaghetti or ropes of pasta.) Lay the finished pasta on a floured baking sheet. (The pasta will keep in the refrigerator for a day or can be frozen for up to a month.)

7  Bring a large pot of salted water to a boil. Add the pasta and cook until just under *al dente*, 2 to 3 minutes, depending on the thickness of the strands. Drain, reserving 1 cup of the cooking water.

8  Return the sauce to a simmer. Add the pasta and cook for 2 to 3 minutes, adding some of the reserved pasta water if the sauce is dry. Serve.

# SPAGHETTI *al* CARTOCCIO

## *Seafood Spaghetti in Parchment Bundles*

I learned about cooking with parchment paper when I was in culinary school in Montecatini. I was so tickled with the technique that I wanted to wrap everything in paper—and I wasn't the only one. Back in the 1980s, chefs were cooking everything from fruit to pasta in parchment. Even though it might just seem like a presentation gimmick, cooking pasta this way gives more flavor to the noodles as they steam in the sauce. Nowadays you can buy premade parchment envelopes or even aluminum foil ones, but I like the old-fashioned way better. Making the envelopes is a little more time-consuming, but they look better on the plate.

SERVES 4

1 pound spaghetti

8 sheets parchment paper

¼ cup extra virgin olive oil

3 teaspoons minced garlic

2 tablespoons finely chopped fresh Italian parsley

10 fresh basil leaves, shredded

1 teaspoon crushed red pepper

1 dozen mussels, scrubbed and debearded

1 dozen Manilla clams, scrubbed

¼ pound cleaned calamari, cut into 1-inch rings

½ pound (12–18 large) shrimp, shelled, deveined, and cut in half lengthwise

½ cup dry white wine

1 cup canned whole tomatoes, with their juice, pureed or crushed (You can use canned pureed or crushed tomatoes, but I think whole ones are less acidic and of higher quality.)

Salt

Freshly ground black pepper

WINE SUGGESTION: *I like a medium-bodied crisp white with this seafood spaghetti dish. Look for Poggio Argentato, which is made made from Sauvignon Blanc and Traminer grapes by Fattoria Le Pupille, a wine grower in Maremma.*

1 Preheat the oven to 350° F. Cut parchment paper into eight 16-inch squares.

2 Bring a large pot of salted water to a boil. Add the spaghetti and cook for 5 minutes. The strands should be very *al dente*, but pliable; they should not break when bent. Drain.

*(continued)*

3 While the pasta is cooking, coat the bottom of a large skillet with the olive oil. Add the garlic, parsley, basil, and crushed red pepper and sauté over medium heat until the garlic begins to color.

4 Add all of the seafood and toss quickly to coat with the oil and herbs. Add the wine, cover, and cook for 2 to 3 minutes.

5 Add the tomatoes and season with salt and pepper to taste. Cover and cook for 5 minutes. Set aside.

6 When the spaghetti is ready, add it to the sauce. Toss to coat, turn off the heat, and reserve.

7 Line a small mixing bowl with two of the parchment squares to create a double layer. Scoop a quarter of the spaghetti and sauce into the center of the square. Gather up the paper and tie it very securely with butcher's twine. Repeat three more times to create 4 pasta "bundles."

8 Put the bundles on a cookie sheet and bake for 5 to 7 minutes. To serve, place each parchment bundle in a pasta bowl. Let each diner untie and open the package to experience the perfume of this combination.

## • BOTTARGA •

Making *bottarga* is almost as labor-intensive as bottling Champagne. After the roe is extracted from the fish, it is brined for different lengths of time, depending on the size of the eggs. Makers then mix the roe with salt in a vat and begin compressing the eggs with weights placed on each container. The mixture is stirred and resalted daily for about three weeks before the roe is rinsed with fresh water and dried in the sun for a day or two. At that point, the roe rests indoors a day before further drying in a ventilated room for two to three months. The *bottarga* is ready when it reaches an intense pink color, almost like raw tuna. While it's thought that the Phoenicians invented this specialty, the Arabs popularized it around the Mediterranean. The most famous places in Italy today where *bottarga* is made are Sicily, Calabria, Maremma, and Sardinia, though the eggs are often imported from Spain, Portugal, and Turkey.

# SPAGHETTI BOTTARGA
## Spaghetti with Bottarga

*Bottarga*, tuna or gray mullet roe that's been dried in salt and pressed into a block, is a kind of very intense caviar and is used to flavor something neutral, like pasta. I think it's addictive. If I see *bottarga* as an ingredient in a dish on a menu anywhere, that's the first dish I order.

**SERVES 4 TO 6**

1 pound spaghetti

½ cup extra virgin olive oil

1½ tablespoons chopped garlic

½ cup chopped fresh Italian parsley

1 teaspoon crushed red pepper

2 tablespoons oven-dried tomatoes

1 ounce *bottarga*, sliced (⅓ cup)
(see Sources on page 221)

**WINE SUGGESTION:** *I'd go with a light, fruity Ansonica, a white wine from the same area where* bottarga *is made. Ansonica is one of the oldest wines in Italy.*

1  Bring a large pot of salted water to a boil, add the spaghetti, and cook until just under *al dente*. Drain, reserving 1 cup of the cooking water.

2  Coat the bottom of a large skillet with the olive oil. Add the garlic and sauté over medium heat for 1 minute.

3  Add the parsley and crushed red pepper. Before the garlic browns, add ½ cup of the reserved pasta cooking water. Let this simmer for 1 minute, then add the tomatoes and cooked pasta. Simmer for 2 to 3 minutes to allow the pasta to absorb the flavor of the sauce. Add a little more water if the mixture seems dry.

4  Toss well and divide among serving plates. Slice the *bottarga* into small, thin uniform pieces over the pasta and serve.

# SPAGHETTI *con* SARDE

## *Spaghetti with Sardines*

I love the legend of spaghetti with sardines almost as much as I love the dish itself. Supposedly the story dates to Byzantine times, when a Greek militia captain fell in love with a Sicilian nun. To avoid getting his nose cut off (punishment for ravishing a nun at the time), the captain left the island. But that wasn't the end of it: He came back for revenge, as the head of an invading Arab army intent upon capturing Syracuse. When his troops landed at Mazara, the captain supposedly ordered his Arab cooks to see what they could find to feed his men. They came back with the ingredients for this dish. In truth, this is more of a Sicilian dish, but we also eat it in Tuscany, along the Arno River. **SERVES 4 TO 6**

1 pound spaghetti

⅓ cup extra virgin olive oil, plus 2 tablespoons

2 tablespoons chopped anchovy fillets (about 8–10) in oil (I prefer the taste of salted anchovies, but they need to be soaked in white wine or water for a few hours or overnight before using.)

1 tablespoon minced garlic

1½ pounds fresh sardine fillets, cleaned, tails removed, and cut into ¾-inch pieces

1 cup diced fennel

¼ cup pine nuts, toasted

¼ cup raisins, soaked in water until softened and drained

Salt

Freshly ground black pepper

¼ cup fennel fronds

¼ cup Bread Crumbs, toasted (page 27)

1 teaspoon fennel pollen (optional, see Sources on page 221)

**WINE SUGGESTION:** *Since this is mostly a Sicilian dish, the best choice for wine would probably be a Sicilian white like Nozze d'Oro, made from Ansonica and Sauvignon grapes. But to give the meal a Tuscan spin, look for one of our Chardonnays. Pomino Benefizio has a nice, clean finish.*

1 Bring a large pot of salted water to a boil. Add the spaghetti and cook until just under *al dente*. Drain, reserving 1 cup of the cooking water.

2 Coat the bottom of a large skillet with the ⅓ cup olive oil. Add the anchovies and sauté over medium heat for 3 minutes, or until the anchovies start to melt. Add the garlic and cook for 1 to 2 minutes.

3 Add the fresh sardines and cook for 3 minutes.

4 Add the diced fennel, pine nuts, and raisins. Add ½ cup of the reserved pasta water and cook for 3 to 4 minutes.

5 Add the spaghetti and cook for 2 to 3 minutes until the pasta absorbs the sauce, adding more pasta water if the mixture is dry. Season with salt and pepper. Stir in three quarters of the fennel fronds and bread crumbs and add the fennel pollen if using. Stir in 1 to 2 tablespoons of the remaining olive oil and thoroughly combine. Transfer to a platter and top with the remaining bread crumbs and fennel fronds.

# SPAGHETTI *con* COZZE
## *Spaghetti with Mussels*

This dish is a staple at almost any seaside resort in Tuscany. Basically it is the same recipe as for spaghetti with clams, just made with mussels. Though many Italians have so much confidence in their mussel supply they eat them raw, I'm a little more squeamish. Make sure the mussels you choose are live by tapping the shell on the countertop. If the mussel doesn't close, discard it. SERVES 4 TO 8

1 pound spaghetti

¼ cup extra virgin olive oil

3 garlic cloves, thinly sliced

2 teaspoons finely chopped fresh thyme

¼ cup finely chopped fresh Italian parsley

1 teaspoon crushed red pepper

2 pounds mussels, scrubbed and debearded

½ cup dry white wine

1 cup canned plum tomatoes, with their juice, crushed or pureed (You can also buy canned crushed or pureed tomatoes, but I think the whole ones are less acidic and of higher quality.)

Salt

Freshly ground black pepper

WINE SUGGESTION: *Ask your wine store for an aromatic red from the Maremma, like Lohsa Mandrione dell'Osa, which is a new wine that's attracting a lot of attenion. I like it because it reminds me of licorice. A good alternative would be Poliziano's Vino Nobile di Montepulciano.*

1 Bring a large pot of salted water to a boil. Add the spaghetti and cook until just under *al dente*. Drain, reserving 1 cup of the cooking water.

2 Coat the bottom of a large skillet with the olive oil. Add the garlic, thyme, half of the parsley, and the crushed red pepper and sauté over medium heat until the garlic starts to color.

3 Add the mussels, wine, and tomatoes. Season with salt and pepper to taste, cover, and cook until the mussels open, 5 to 7 minutes.

4 When the spaghetti is ready, add it to the sauce with ½ cup to 1 cup of the pasta cooking water (depending how dry the sauce is). Cook the spaghetti in the sauce, uncovered, for 2 to 3 minutes for the pasta to absorb the sauce. Stir in the remaining parsley and serve.

# • ROSA AND PIETRO •

You probably wouldn't be surprised if I told you that my parents, Rosa and Pietro Casella, are the reason I'm a chef. But even though they had their own restaurant, Vipore, outside of Lucca, and raised me in the kitchen, they did everything to keep me from going into the family business, including trying to bribe me into applying to law school by buying me a bright yellow Fiat 500. Their opposition only made me want to be a chef even more.

That's the short version, anyway. As I think about it now, I didn't really have a choice. Cooking was the life I grew up with, and I was weaned on rosemary and garlic and slow roasted pork. Traditional tastes and smells became a part of me. Plus, my parents were fanatics and I couldn't help but absorb their passion. For my dad, it was all about ingredients. I remember driving three or four hours with him just to find a great box of porcini mushrooms. For a few years, he actually cornered the porcini market near us, buying all the mushrooms in the area, keeping the best for Vipore and then selling the leftovers to small grocers. And when we went to visit the mushroom pickers, we always traveled with gifts of salami and wine to ensure they'd give us their prime goods.

My mom, on the other hand, chased me out of the kitchen to discourage my curiosity, but really, she's the one who taught me how to cook. I'd spy on her when she wasn't paying attention, absorbing everything, from how to clean thyme to dressing a piece of meat. It wasn't until I graduated from cooking school and started working side by side with her at Vipore that my mom accepted that I was going to be a chef. Then she'd talk to me for hours about food. To help me learn the restaurant business in and out, she insisted that I work with her in the kitchen until about six P.M., then move to the dining room to meet and greet customers. I always suspected her real motive was to make clear who was in charge of the kitchen, and that was okay by me.

# SALSA *di* NORCINO
## *Butcher's Pasta*

Back in the old days, a *norcino* was the butcher—from the town of Norcia—who traveled from house to house making sausage for pig farmers. I call this dish the butcher's spaghetti because, to me, it's all about the sausage. No other meat can compete with the fat and flavor of a well-fed pig. That statement goes doubly for sausage, which I think of as a complete food group. This dish is so easy to make that it is almost foolproof. **SERVES 4 TO 6**

2 tablespoons roughly chopped garlic

1½ cups roughly chopped red onions

2 cups roughly chopped celery

¼ cup extra virgin olive oil

1 tablespoon finely chopped fresh rosemary

2½ pounds hot sausage, casings removed and meat crumbled

2½ pounds sweet sausage, casings removed and meat crumbled

1 cup dry red wine

3½ cups canned whole tomatoes, with their juice, pureed or finely chopped (You can also buy pureed tomatoes, but whole ones are less acidic and of higher quality.)

Large pinch crushed red pepper

Large pinch grated nutmeg

Large pinch ground cloves

Large pinch ground cinnamon

Salt

Freshly ground black pepper

1 pound spaghetti

Grated Parmesan cheese, for finishing

**WINE SUGGESTION:** *With the spices in this pasta, I like a Grognolo, which is a blend of Sangiovese and Merlot grapes. This well-structured wine tastes of blackberries.*

1  In a food processor puree the garlic, onions, and celery to a coarse paste.

2  Coat the bottom of a large skillet with the olive oil. Add the garlic and onion paste and the rosemary and sauté over medium heat until the mixture begins to color, 10 to 15 minutes.

3  Add the sausage meats, stirring with a wooden spoon to break them up. When the sausage is brown, add the wine and reduce completely, 8 to 10 minutes.

**4** Add the tomatoes, crushed red pepper, nutmeg, cloves, cinnamon, and 4 cups water. Season with salt and pepper. Cook over low heat for 3 hours, adding additional water, a little at a time, if the mixture starts to look too dry. When the sauce is ready, skim off the excess fat and adjust the seasonings.

**5** Bring a large pot of salted water to a boil. Add the spaghetti and cook until just under *al dente*. Drain, reserving 1 cup of the cooking water.

**6** Add the spaghetti to the sauce with ½ cup of the cooking water. Continue cooking 2 to 3 minutes for the pasta to absorb some of the sauce, adding more pasta water if the mixture becomes too dry. Sprinkle with the Parmesan and serve.

# PASTA *al* CINGHIALE
## *Wild Boar Pasta*

This is a variation on the Wild Boar Gnocchi I make (page 71). Instead of incorporating the meat into the dough as I do in that recipe, here I toss the sauce with pasta and top it with Parmesan. If you can't find wild boar, pork shoulder or butt will do as a substitute.

SERVES 4 TO 6

2 pounds wild boar, cut into ¾-inch chunks (or pork shoulder or pork butt)

Salt

Freshly ground black pepper

½ cup flour

½ cup extra virgin olive oil

3 cups roughly chopped onions

2 cups roughly chopped carrots

4 cups roughly chopped celery

3 garlic cloves

1½ teaspoons crushed red pepper

4 cups strong red wine

7–8 juniper berries

3 bay leaves

1 sprig fresh rosemary

1 sprig fresh sage leaves

3 cups vegetable stock

3 cups canned whole tomatoes, drained and pureed (You can use canned pureed tomatoes, but I think the whole ones are less acidic and of higher quality.)

¼ cup unsweetened cocoa powder, less or more, to taste

1 teaspoon freshly ground black pepper

¼ to ⅓ teaspoon Tuscan Spice (see Sources on page 221), or *garam masala*, or mix together equal parts ground allspice, cinnamon, nutmeg, and cloves

1 pound short pasta, such as penne

⅓ cup grated Parmesan cheese, for finishing

WINE SUGGESTION: *This is a traditional dish and I like it with Avvoltore, a more complex red wine from Morisfarms in the Maremma.*

1 Sprinkle the meat liberally with salt and pepper. Dredge the meat in the flour, shaking off the excess.

2 Coat the bottom of a large pot with ¼ cup of the olive oil and heat over medium-high heat. Add the meat to the hot oil and brown on all sides. If the pan isn't big enough for the meat to fit in a single layer, brown the meat in two batches, draining off the fat and wiping the pan after the first batch. Remove the meat from the pot and set aside.

3 In a food processor pulse the onions, carrots, celery, and garlic together until finely chopped but not pureed.

4 Add the remaining ¼ cup olive oil, chopped vegetables, and crushed red pepper to the pot and sauté over medium-high heat until the mixture begins to color, 10 to 12 minutes. Return the meat to the pot, stir well, and cook for 3 to 4 minutes.

5 Add the wine and reduce it by three quarters.

6 Tie the juniper berries, bay leaves, and rosemary and sage sprigs in a 6-inch square piece of cheesecloth. Add to the sauce with the vegetable stock and tomatoes. Stir in the cocoa powder, Tuscan spice, and more salt and pepper to taste. Stir well to combine and to dissolve any lumps of cocoa powder. Cover and simmer for 2 hours, or until the meat is falling apart. Remove cheesecloth bag.

7 Transfer half of the sauce to a food processor and puree. Return the puree to the pot, cover, and simmer 20 minutes.

8 Meanwhile, bring a large pot of salted water to a boil. Add the penne and cook until just under *al dente*. Drain, reserving 1 cup of the cooking liquid.

9 Add the pasta to the sauce and simmer 2 to 3 minutes, adding ½ cup of the pasta water if the mixture seems dry. Add more water as necessary. Remove the pasta from the heat, sprinkle with the Parmesan, and combine well. Serve.

# TESTAROLI

## Tuscan Crepes with Wild Mushroom Sauce

I've made a lot of unusual pastas, but this is the one that surprises people the most, especially when they hear how it's made. Basically *testaroli* are thin pancakes that you slice into strips and boil like pasta. They sound odd, but they're delicious; just ask the legions of people from Lunigiana (on the border between Tuscany and Liguria) who have eaten them for centuries. The name comes from the *testo*, which is the cast-iron griddle the pancakes are cooked on—a pot so popular in Lunigiana in the Middle Ages that there was a tax on it. Some people think that *testaroli* were the forerunners to pasta, but I'm not speculating. They are great with mushrooms, though. SERVES 4 TO 6

3½ cups all-purpose flour

1 teaspoon salt, plus more to taste

Freshly ground black pepper

¼ cup extra virgin olive oil, plus more for drizzling

2 tablespoons minced garlic

1 tablespoon finely chopped fresh oregano

2 tablespoons finely chopped fresh Italian parsley

2 pounds mixed mushrooms (cremini, shiitake, oyster, chanterelle, or button), cleaned and thinly sliced

2 cups canned whole tomatoes, with their juice, pureed or crushed (You can also use pureed or crushed canned tomatoes, but I think whole ones are less acidic and of higher quality.)

1½ cups vegetable stock or water

Bacon fat, for cooking (or peanut oil for a lighter taste)

½ cup grated Parmesan cheese

WINE SUGGESTION: *There's a wine with a history that goes back hundreds of years that I love, Massaretta, which comes from the same area as* testaroli *and goes really well with this mushroom dish. Look for the producer Aurelio Cima.*

1  In a large bowl combine the flour, 1 teaspoon salt, and a pinch of pepper.

2  Add water, 1 cup at a time, until a thin batter has formed. You should not need more than 3 cups. Whisk until there are no lumps. Let the batter stand for 2 hours.

**3** Meanwhile, coat the bottom of a large skillet with the ¼ cup olive oil. Add the garlic and sauté over medium heat until it begins to color. Add the oregano and parsley and cook for 1 minute.

**4** Add the mushrooms and season with salt and pepper to taste. (Add more oil if the mushrooms seem dry.) Cook for 7 to 8 minutes, or until the mushrooms are very soft.

**5** Add the tomatoes with the vegetable stock or water. Season with salt and pepper. Bring to a simmer and cook for 25 to 30 minutes, stirring occasionally. Adjust the seasoning and set the sauce aside.

**6** After the batter has rested for 2 hours, place 1 teaspoon of bacon fat or peanut oil in an 8-inch nonstick sauté pan over medium heat. (A nonstick pan makes it easier to flip the *testaroli*, but you can also use an untreated pan.) Tilt the pan to distribute the fat and pour off the excess. Pour ¼ cup of the batter into the center of the pan. Cook until firm and slightly brown on one side, 2 to 3 minutes, flip, and cook on the other side. If the batter puffs up, press down gently with the back of a fork to release the steam. Remove the pancake to a plate. Repeat until all of the batter is used. Stack the pancakes between paper towels and let cool completely.

**7** Bring a large pot of well-salted water to a boil. Meanwhile, slice the pasta pancakes into ½-inch strips. Cut each strip diagonally into 1-inch lengths. Add the pasta to the boiling water and cook for about 1 minute, or until all the pieces have floated to the top. Drain, reserving 1 cup of the cooking water. Reheat the mushroom sauce to just under a simmer. Add the pasta strips, stir to coat well, and add ½ cup of the cooking water or more if needed to thin the mixture. Sprinkle with the grated Parmesan and drizzle with olive oil. Serve.

# RISOTTO *della* LUNIGIANA
## *Mushroom, Sausage, and Artichoke Risotto*

The summer I was thirteen my father started taking me to Lunigiana, an area where Tuscany borders Liguria and Emilia Romagna. He made the trip to buy fresh porcini and Parmesan cheese, but I went along because it was the only place to find this version of risotto. To make it, I recommend cremini or shiitake mushrooms, since fresh porcini are almost impossible to find here. In fact, the recipe is relatively adaptable, though I have provided the full list of ingredients. Most people omit something, and you can swap fresh artichokes for frozen hearts. Just don't leave out the sausage and the porcini. **SERVES 4 TO 6**

1 lemon

3 ounces (1 cup) baby artichokes (or globe artichoke bottoms and hearts or frozen artichoke hearts)

4 tablespoons extra virgin olive oil

1 cup thinly sliced onions

1 tablespoon minced garlic

¼ cup finely chopped fresh Italian parsley

½ pound Italian sausage links, casings removed and crumbled

½ pound fresh porcini, cremini, or shiitake mushrooms, sliced

2 quarts chicken stock (page 66)

2 cups Carnaroli or Arborio rice

¾ cup dry white wine

1 cup green peas, fresh or frozen

Salt

Fresh ground black pepper

1 tablespoon butter

2 tablespoons grated Parmesan cheese

---

**WINE SUGGESTION:** *It might be hard to track one down, but look for a wine from Lunigiana; otherwise, go with a Tuscan Chardonnay, or a light young red, served chilled, like Casamatta, which is made from Sangiovese grapes.*

---

1   Fill a bowl with water. Cut the lemon in half and squeeze the juice into the water. Add the squeezed lemon halves to the water, too. If you are using baby artichokes, peel the outer leaves from the artichokes until you reach the part where the leaves are mostly a creamy yellow. Cut the top inch off the artichoke and trim away the stem so that you are left with a golf ball-sized heart. Quarter the hearts and put in the acidulated water. (For globe artichokes, remove the tough outer leaves and cut the artichokes into wedges. Remove the choke and the soft curly leaves above it. Put in the water.) Set aside.

2  Coat the bottom of a large skillet with the olive oil. Add the sliced onions, garlic, and 2 tablespoons of the parsley and sauté over medium heat until the garlic starts to color, about 5 minutes.

3  Add the sausage and mushrooms, to the skillet and sauté until the sausage is cooked through and slightly brown, 4 to 5 minutes.

4  Bring the chicken stock to a simmer in a saucepan and turn off the heat.

5  Add the rice to the skillet and toast for 5 to 6 minutes, stirring constantly to prevent sticking and burning. Drain the artichokes. Add them, along with the wine. Cook, stirring frequently, until the rice absorbs all of the wine.

6  Add enough warm chicken stock to cover the rice and cook stirring frequently, until the chicken stock has absorbed the rice. Repeat this step with the chicken stock two more times, adding the peas after the rice has cooked for 15 minutes. Check the doneness of the rice, add a little more chicken stock, and cook a little longer if needed. Adjust the seasonings.

7  When the rice is cooked to the proper consistency, firm but not crunchy, turn off the heat. Stir in the butter, Parmesan, and remaining 2 tablespoons parsley. Serve immediately.

# FARROTTO *con* ZUCCA

## *Farro with Squash and Kale*

During the Ides of March, the Romans used to offer Demetra, the Earth Goddess, farro to bring a good harvest. To me, this barleylike grain is all that's good about food: Farro is rich and hearty and tastes like the earth. Although it's hard to claim invention in the kitchen, I like to think that I invented this dish, now known as "farrotto" (*farro* is Italian for spelt). I add everything from seafood to duck to it, but this black kale and squash version is my favorite. **SERVES 4 TO 6**

½ pound black kale (5 cups) or regular kale

½ cup extra virgin olive oil

1 tablespoon chopped garlic

1 teaspoon crushed red pepper

8 cups squash chunks, such as butternut, kurry and/or delakuta varieties

1 tablespoon chopped fresh sage

4 quarts vegetable stock or water (stock is preferable)

1 cup chopped red onions

2½ cups farro (also called spelt; available in health food stores)

½ cup grated Parmesan cheese

---

**WINE SUGGESTION:** *A perfect match for this dish is Poggio alla Badiola, a simple, soft wine that's mostly of the Sangiovese grape.*

---

1 Wash the kale and pull the leaves off the ribs. Chop leaves and cut the ribs into 1-inch pieces.

2 Coat the bottom of a stockpot with ¼ cup of the olive oil. Add the garlic and crushed red pepper and sauté over medium heat until the garlic starts to color. Add the kale, squash, sage, and 2 quarts of the vegetable stock or water. Bring to a simmer and cook for 30 minutes.

3 Add 2 cups of the stock or water and simmer for another 30 to 45 minutes until the squash is cooked through. Remove the pan from the heat.

**4** Coat the bottom of another large skillet with the remaining ¼ cup olive oil. Add the chopped onions and sauté over medium heat until translucent, 8 to 10 minutes. Add the farro, stirring frequently, and cook for 5 minutes.

**5** Add 1 cup of the remaining vegetable stock and cook until it is absorbed; continue adding the remaining stock, 1 cup at a time, until all liquid has been absorbed and the farro is *al dente*. You might not use all of the liquid; you need to judge when the farro is plump. It should take about 30 minutes.

**6** Add the kale and squash mixture to the skillet and cook until well combined and creamy, about 30 minutes.

**7** Sprinkle the mixture with the Parmesan and serve immediately.

# SECONDI

## Seafood, Poultry, and Meats

I like to think creatively when I cook. Take the ribs I describe as Tuscan cowboy style. You won't find this recipe in any Italian cookbook, Tuscan or otherwise. But it is quintessentially Italian for me. For one, it's inspired by the Tuscan cowboys who herd cattle in the Maremma. The recipe also makes use of the traditional *alla cacciatora* way of stewing chicken or rabbit in tomato sauce. Still, ribs like this would be pretty unusual in Tuscany, and even more so paired with broccoli rabe, a vegetable you mostly see in the south of Italy. But I like trying new things.

While Italians in Italy tend to be very strict about what flavors can be mixed and matched, creativity crops up subtly. It could be a secret ingredient, like a splash of lemon juice or a pinch of cinnamon that is difficult to identify. Or it could be a heating technique, such as finishing a dish over very high heat or cooling it down over a bowl of ice. For instance, there probably aren't two identical recipes for *stracotto*, our version of pot roast, in the entire country. Every area has its own version. Same with fish soup. And you'll never guess why: During the Middle Ages, when all the city states were warring with each other, there was little communication or trade among regions, so each area developed its own unique cuisine.

Another way Italians are creative is with the presentation and order of courses. While Americans tend to organize meals like jigsaw puzzles, fitting a meat, starch, and vegetable together on a plate, in Italy we see each dish as a stand-alone item. It's a slightly more free-form approach, giving the diner almost as much control as the cook, since the diner decides what to eat. In this way, the *secondo* is less the centerpiece of the meal than it is a component. Often people skip a *secondo* and just have a *primo*, or vice versa. Dishes Americans might consider strictly main courses become *primi* simply by being served in smaller portions. The idea to keep in mind is, as always, flexibility.

# CACCIUCCO

## *Tuscan Fish Stew*

In Tuscany, someone in a *cacciucco* is in a real muddle. Perhaps this soup is a fish muddle, just one with great, deep flavors. *Cacciucco* has a different twist depending upon where you are: In Livorno, it's very spicy; in Versilia, sweet. Aside from really fresh fish of any kind, the key ingredients are red pepper, black pepper, garlic, salt, and herbs. Using red wine will make the dish more robust. I like to remove the clams and mussels from the shells to make eating the stew easier. Leave in a few, though, to scoop up the broth.

On a separate note, if you want to make your own simple fish stock, buy 2 pounds of fish bones when you're purchasing your fish; wash them, put them in a pot with 3 quarts water, and simmer for 1 hour. **SERVES 6**

1½ cups onion chunks

1 cup celery chunks

½ cup carrot chunks

2 tablespoons sliced garlic, plus 2 whole cloves

1 teaspoon crushed red pepper

2 tablespoons chopped fresh Italian parsley

5 sage leaves

3 tablespoons extra virgin olive oil

½ pound squid or cuttlefish, cut into strips

1 cup dry white wine

2 cups canned whole tomatoes, with their juice, pureed (You can use canned pureed tomatoes, but I think the whole ones are less acidic and of higher quality.)

A 1-pound grouper or red snapper, cleaned and cut into 2-inch cubes

½ pound (12 medium) peeled shrimp

1¼ pounds (about 30) mussels, scrubbed and debearded

1½ pounds (about 2 dozen) small clams, scrubbed

4 cups fish stock (see headnote) or vegetable stock

Salt

Freshly ground black pepper

6 slices thick crusty bread

**WINE SUGGESTION:** *There is so much going on in this stew, I like to serve a really simple red, like a Rosso di Montalcino or a Chianti. Another light-bodied choice would be a Ciliegiolo, a wine that's usually used for blending, but one that can also be great on its own. Try Poggio Ciliegio from the Cecconello Estate.*

1 Put the onion, celery, carrot, garlic, crushed red pepper, parsley, and sage in a food processor and puree to a coarse paste.

2 Coat the bottom of a stockpot with the olive oil. Add the pureed vegetables and sauté over medium heat until they become soft and very aromatic, 10 to 15 minutes.

3 Add the squid and cook until it turns white, 2 to 3 minutes.

4 Add the wine and reduce by half.

5 Add the tomatoes, fish, and the stock. Season with salt and a generous grind of pepper. Bring the soup to a simmer and cook for 10 minutes. Add the shellfish and cook for 10 minutes more. Taste for seasoning. Discard any shellfish that did not open.

6 Toast the bread and rub it with the whole garlic cloves. Put a toast in the bottom of each soup bowl and ladle soup over it.

# BORDATINO di MARE

## Polenta with Seafood

I know being a galley cook on a ship was hard work, but there's something romantic about it to me—especially the making of the *bordatino,* or on-board meal. From accounts I've read, the cook worked with a pot sitting on a tripod (for more stability and fewer spills) and rummaged the storeroom for ingredients to add to a runny polenta—from oil infused with garlic to preserved tomatoes, pancetta, garlic, red pepper, or some dried fish like anchovies or salt cod. Polenta was used instead of pasta because the cornmeal kept better once made than pasta did. If a mate happened to catch something fresh, the cook would roast it and serve it with the polenta. **SERVES** 6

2 cups fish stock (page 120)

7 sage leaves

¼ cup extra virgin olive oil

Salt

1½ cups polenta (be sure it is the long-cooking variety, not the instant)

4 teaspoons minced garlic

2 tablespoons anchovy fillets (about 6) in oil (I prefer the taste of salted anchovies, but they need to be soaked in white wine or water for a few hours or overnight before using.)

½ teaspoon crushed red pepper

3 tablespoons chopped fresh Italian parsley

½ cup dry white wine

¾ pound grouper fillets (skin removed), or any fish that you like, cut into bite-size pieces

Freshly ground black pepper

½ cup grated Parmesan cheese

---

**WINE SUGGESTION:** *My first choice would actually be a sweeter than usual beer, like Moretti Rossa. But you can't go wrong with il Templare made by Montenidoli, from Verdicchio, Vermentimo, Vernaccia, Trebbiamo, Malvasia and Grechetto grapes.*

---

1 Combine 6 cups water and the fish stock in a stockpot. Scoop out a cup of the liquid and set it aside (or just use 5 cups water). Bring to a boil. Add the sage leaves, 2 tablespoons of the olive oil, and salt to taste. Stir the polenta into the water and simmer over low heat for 45 minutes. Stir occasionally to prevent the polenta from sticking.

2 Coat the bottom of a large skillet with the remaining 2 tablespoons olive oil. Add the garlic, anchovies, crushed red pepper, and parsley and sauté over medium heat until the garlic begins to color. Add the wine and cook until reduced by half.

3 Season the fish with salt and pepper and add it to the skillet. Cook until the fish becomes opaque, about 10 minutes.

4 Add the fish mixture to the polenta, stirring well. Stir in the Parmesan. The consistency should be like very loose cream of wheat. Pour the polenta into a large serving tureen. Use the reserved liquid to loosen any polenta that sticks to the pot and add to the tureen. Taste for seasoning and serve.

# CUSCUSSO *di* MARE
## *Seafood Couscous*

Couscous has been a staple food in the port of Livorno since the 1500s, when the king at the time invited foreigners to repopulate the city after a malaria epidemic wiped out much of the local citizenry. Some of the immigrants were Sephardic Jews, who'd been kicked out of Spain during the Inquisition and were attracted by the fact that Livorno already had a sizable Jewish population. The Jews arrived with a variety of recipes and foods, including the tomato. Though the most typical Jewish version of couscous was made with squash, onions, carrots, and tiny lamb meatballs, over time the Livornese turned it into a seafood dish, which is how I like to make it. **SERVES 4**

A 1-pound octopus, cleaned

2 tablespoons red wine vinegar

1 whole carrot

1 medium red onion, quartered, plus 1¼ cups thinly sliced red onions

Salt

½ pound fish fillets, skin removed; any kind, cut into bite-size pieces

½ pound calamari, cut lengthwise into ¼-inch strips

2 dozen mussels, scrubbed and debearded

2 dozen manila clams

½ pound large shrimp, shelled and cut in half lengthwise

1 cup diced butternut squash

¼ pound Swiss chard, washed, stems cut into 1-inch lengths, and leaves chopped (about 2 cups)

1½ cups cooked chick-peas (page 187)

½ cup dry white wine

1 teaspoon crushed red pepper

¼ cup extra virgin olive oil

2 garlic cloves, sliced

2 sprigs fresh thyme

2 tablespoons harissa sauce (a very hot pepper sauce, available in specialty and Middle Eastern markets)

2 cups hot fish stock (page 120)

Pinch saffron (optional)

1 cup instant couscous

Freshly ground black pepper

1  Put the octopus in a large stockpot with enough water to cover by 4 inches, and add the vinegar, carrot, quartered red onion, and salt. Bring to a simmer and cook for 45 minutes, or until the octopus is tender. Let cool and drain, discarding carrot and onion. Cut the octopus into bite-size pieces.

WINE SUGGESTION: *Montalcino is mostly known in the United States for its red wines, but it also makes some very good whites. With this couscous, I'd try a white wine from Montalcino, like Le Rime, a Pinot Grigio, or a Chardonnay with some Pinot in it.*

2  Combine the octopus, fish, calamari, mussels, clams, shrimp, squash, Swiss chard, chick-peas, and wine in a large bowl. Season with salt and the crushed red pepper.

3  Coat the bottom of a large skillet with the olive oil. Add the sliced red onions, garlic, and thyme sprigs and sauté over medium heat until the garlic starts to color, about 5 minutes. Add the seafood and chick-pea mixture and combine well. Cover tightly with a lid and cook for 5 minutes.

4  In a bowl stir together the harissa sauce, hot fish stock, saffron if using, and salt and pepper to taste. Add to the skillet and stir to combine. Add the couscous, stir well, cover, and remove the pan from the heat. Let stand until all of the liquid has been absorbed by the couscous, 4 to 5 minutes. Taste for seasoning and serve immediately.

# GAMBERONI *alla* MODA
## *della* CUCINA

### *Kitchen Shrimp*

I have a lot of Ecuadorian cooks in my restaurant kitchen and when we have the family meal before service, they douse their food with a spicy sauce they bring from home. From the first time I tasted it, I loved its fiery flavor and thought it would give a kick to a plate of shrimp. Though this isn't a traditional Tuscan dish, it's so simple I think of it as Tuscan in spirit. In Tuscany, we'd probably use crushed red pepper instead of jalapeño and parsley instead of cilantro, and you should try that variation, too. This is now one of my favorite dishes. I serve it with an arugula and tomato salad. **SERVES 4 TO 6**

3 tablespoons minced jalapeño pepper, seeds removed

1 cup diced fresh tomatoes (no need to peel)

3 tablespoons minced cilantro

Salt

Freshly ground black pepper

5 tablespoons extra virgin olive oil

2 pounds large shrimp, deveined, but shells left intact

**WINE SUGGESTION:** *Honestly, I eat these shrimp with Corona beer, but if you're set on wine, try a Tuscan Gewürztraminer from San Vettore, a vineyard near San Gimignano.*

1 Combine all of the ingredients except the shrimp in a large bowl and combine well. (I add at least 1 teaspoon black pepper. Add as much as you like.)

2 Butterfly the shrimp, leaving the shells intact, and put in a large bowl. Pour the tomato marinade over the shrimp and refrigerate for at least ½ hour or up to 24 hours.

3 Prepare the grill on the highest setting or preheat the broiler.

4 Grill the shrimp, shell side down, for 5 to 7 minutes. Serve hot. If broiling, arrange the shrimp on a sizzle platter or baking sheet and broil about 5 inches from the heat, moving the sheet every few minutes until the shrimp are ready, 5 to 10 minutes, depending how hot the broiler is. Serve at once.

# GAMBERONI *in* GUAZZETTO

## *Jumbo Shrimp, Maremma-style*

Some versions of this dish in old Italian cookbooks call for *datteri*, or dates, wording I love, because it's also Livornese slang for a certain type of clam. Fishing for *datteri* is now outlawed (it requires severing the mollusk from the rock with a knife), so modern recipes use clams called truffles because their firm, but soft texture is a little like truffles. Here I prefer shrimp, which I think go perfectly with the spicy tomato sauce. If the sauce is too hot for you, tone it down a notch with less pepper. **SERVES 4**

3 tablespoons extra virgin olive oil

5 garlic cloves, crushed and left in big pieces

3 tablespoons chopped fresh Italian parsley

1 teaspoon crushed red pepper

1 cup dry white wine

1½ pounds (24) jumbo shrimp, shelled and deveined

1 cup fresh tomato chunks (no need to peel)

1 tablespoon torn basil leaves

Salt

Freshly ground black pepper

4 slices thick crusty bread, toasted

---

**WINE SUGGESTION:** *In Maremma, vintners often blend the Alicante and Sangiovese grapes for a dark fruity red. These wines will pick up perfectly on the tomato sauce. If you can find such a bottle, look for an Alicante Querciolaia from Mantellassi.*

---

1  Coat the bottom of a large skillet with the olive oil. Add the garlic, parsley, and red pepper flakes and sauté over medium heat until the garlic starts to color.

2  Add the wine and cook until reduced by half.

3  Add the shrimp, tomatoes, and basil. Cover and cook for 5 to 7 minutes, or just until the shrimp are cooked through. Taste for seasoning and serve the shrimp spooned over or next to the toasts.

# ARAGOSTA FRA DIAVOLA

## *Tuscan Lobster*

I'm not sure, but I think the term *fra diavolo* comes from a famous Italian bandit and soldier, who went by the name Fra Diavolo (friar devil) who was captured and hung by the French in 1806. My guess is that since Sig. Diavolo (his real name was Michele Pezza) was such a provocative guy, his name got attached to spicy dishes. This dish, a very traditional one from the area called Maremma, is all about heat. If your palate is less fireproof than mine, cut down on the red pepper. **SERVES 4**

1 carrot, roughly chopped

1 onion, roughly chopped

1 celery stalk, roughly chopped

Salt

Three 1¼-pound lobsters

¼ cup extra virgin olive oil

4 teaspoons minced garlic

1 teaspoon crushed red pepper

3 tablespoons finely chopped fresh Italian parsley

¼ cup dry white wine

¼ cup brandy or cognac

3 cups canned whole tomatoes, with their juice, pureed (You can use canned pureed tomatoes, but I think the whole ones are less acidic and of higher quality.)

Freshly ground black pepper

1 pound spaghetti

---

**WINE SUGGESTION:** *I like the freshness of a Chardonnay or fizzy white wine with this dish; if you want a light red, the maker Enrico Fossi has a nice one called Sangioveto.*

---

1  Fill a large stockpot with water and add the carrot, onion, celery, and salt to taste. Bring the water to a boil and add the lobsters. As soon as the water returns to a boil, remove the lobsters from the pot and let cool. Reserve the lobster cooking water.

2  When the lobsters are cool enough to handle, remove the meat and cut it into bite-size pieces. Set aside. Return the shells to the lobster cooking water and simmer for 30 minutes. Remove and set aside.

3 Coat the bottom of a large skillet with the olive oil. Add the garlic, crushed red pepper, and 1 tablespoon of the parsley and sauté over medium heat until the garlic begins to color and is very aromatic.

4 Add the wine and brandy and reduce by half. Add the tomatoes and 2 cups of the lobster cooking water. Season with salt and pepper and simmer for 20 minutes.

5 Meanwhile, bring a large pot of salted water to a boil. Add the spaghetti and cook until it is *al dente*. Drain.

6 Add the pasta to the tomato sauce and simmer 1 to 2 minutes, adding a little of the reserved lobster cooking water if needed. Stir in the lobster meat and the remaining 2 tablespoons parsley. Serve immediately, using the lobster shells as a garnish.

# TRIGLIE *al* PROSCIUTTO

## *Red Mullet with Prosciutto*

For the Romans, red mullet was the ultimate in fish—the most tender and the tastiest variety. Though the fish are small, usually just three to six inches long, the Romans managed to remove the livers to use in the famous fermented fish sauce, garum.

Travel anywhere in Europe and you'll find red mullet on restaurant menus, but for some reason the fish never caught on here in America, probably because they're mostly only available on the East Coast and in the Florida Keys. Though the fish are very bony, they're worth the effort. If you have the time, let the fish marinate in the lemon juice and olive oil for an hour or so for even more flavor. **SERVES 4**

3 pounds red mullet (12 fish), butterflied, with spine and pinbones removed, but heads left on (ask your fishmonger to do this)

Salt

Freshly ground black pepper

5 tablespoons extra virgin olive oil

¼ cup lemon juice

8 sprigs fresh thyme

10–12 ounces prosciutto, cut into 24 very thin, large slices

¼ cup Bread Crumbs (page 27)

5 teaspoons minced garlic

2 teaspoons finely chopped fresh Italian parsley

---

**WINE SUGGESTION:** *Sauvignon Blanc is the way to go here. Alternatively, try Bianco di Montecarlo, which is made by my close friend (and restaurateur) Romano Franceschini, from Sauvignon, Semillon, and Roussanne grapes.*

---

1  Preheat the oven to 375° F.

2  If your fishmonger hasn't already done so, trim off the fins and tail on each red mullet with a sharp pair of scissors. (Don't skip this step, or the fish will burn.)

3  Sprinkle the inside of the fish with salt and pepper to taste, 1½ tablespoons of the olive oil, and 2 tablespoons of the lemon juice. Place 1 sprig of thyme in each fish and fold it over to close.

4 Cut each slice of prosciutto in half crosswise and wrap the body of each fish with the halved prosciutto slice.

5 In a large bowl combine the bread crumbs, garlic, parsley, and salt and pepper to taste.

6 Coat the bottom of a baking dish with 2 tablespoons of the remaining olive oil and sprinkle with about half the crumb mixture. Arrange the fish in an even layer in the dish and sprinkle them with the remaining crumb mixture. Drizzle the remaining olive oil and lemon juice over the fish. Bake until the crumbs are golden brown, 10 to 12 minutes. Serve at once.

# TRIGLIE alla MOSAICA
## Mosaic of Red Mullet

This is the way you'll find red mullet cooked in the Jewish quarter of Livorno, both today and one hundred years ago. I'm not sure, but I think it's called "mosaic" because the mullet are served over tomatoes and the tomatoes are arranged mosaic-style on a plate. The locals also call this dish *triglie alla Livornese* and leave the bones in; I prefer a boneless rendition. Red snapper or another delicate white fish makes a good substitute if you can't find red mullet. I enjoy serving this with polenta or mashed potatoes. **SERVES 4**

1 cup chopped red onions

2 cups roughly chopped celery

2 tablespoons roughly chopped garlic

3 sage leaves

2 tablespoons chopped fresh Italian parsley

3 tablespoons extra virgin olive oil

Pinch crushed red pepper

½ cup dry white wine

Salt

Freshly ground black pepper

2 cups whole tomatoes, pureed (You can use canned crushed tomatoes, but I think the whole ones are less acidic and of higher quality.)

2 pounds red mullet fillets

**WINE SUGGESTION**: *I'm all for a rosé with mullet prepared this way, because it brings out the best in the fish. A slightly chilled light red is another good choice, like Sassotondo Ciliegiolo-Alicante blend.*

1 In a food processor puree the onions, celery, garlic, sage leaves, and Italian parsley to a coarse paste. Set aside.

2 Coat the bottom of a large skillet with the olive oil. Add the crushed red pepper and the pureed vegetables and sauté until they become very soft and aromatic, 10 to 15 minutes.

3 Add the wine and season with salt and pepper. Reduce the wine by half.

4 Add the tomatoes and simmer the sauce for 20 to 25 minutes.

5 Season the fish fillets with salt and pepper. Arrange them on the tomato sauce, cover, and simmer until the fish are cooked through, about 10 minutes. Taste for seasoning and serve.

# SALTIMBOCCA *di* PESCATRICE

## *Monkfish with Prosciutto*

When I was in culinary school, one dish our teachers insisted we perfect was *aragosta bellavista*, an elaborate banquet preparation that involved arranging lobster medallions, truffles, and other delicacies on top of a mountain of lobster shells. Since the administration was always trying to make ends meet, we practiced on a molded sculpture of lobster shells and in place of the meat, we used monkfish, which back then was considered the poor man's lobster. It was my first experience with monkfish and I've loved it ever since. The rich texture of the fish is especially good in this recipe as a counterpoint to the prosciutto and bacon. SERVES 4 TO 6

2½ pounds monkfish, cut into 8 fillets

Salt

Freshly ground black pepper

½ pound prosciutto, cut in large thin slices

2 tablespoons chopped fresh sage

1 pound escarole, chopped (6 cups)

1 cup extra virgin olive oil

½ pound bacon, diced (1 cup)

1 tablespoon minced garlic

¼ cup bean cooking water, plus 1 cup cooked cannellini beans (page 187)

Pinch crushed red pepper

WINE SUGGESTION: *I always have this dish with a Tuscan Chardonnay. A good place to start would be Vigna Regis from Vecchie Terre di Monlefili. A light Pinot Nero would be another good option.*

1 Preheat the oven to 375° F.

2 Season each fillet lightly with salt and pepper. Lay a slice of prosciutto on a cutting board and place a monkfish fillet in the middle of it. Sprinkle the fish with a pinch of sage, then wrap the fish in the prosciutto. (If the slices aren't large enough, you might need more than one slice per fillet.) Repeat with all fillets. Set aside.

3 Prepare a bowl of ice water.

*(continued)*

4 Bring a pot of salted water to a boil, add the escarole, and cook 3 to 4 minutes, or until wilted. Drain, transfer to the ice water, and cool for 2 to 3 minutes. Squeeze out the excess water and set aside.

5 Coat the bottom of a large ovenproof skillet with ½ cup of the olive oil and heat over medium-high heat. Add the fillet bundles and brown on all sides. Transfer the skillet to the oven and bake for 10 to 12 minutes.

6 Meanwhile, coat the bottom of a large skillet with the remaining ½ cup olive oil and add the bacon. Sauté over medium heat for 5 minutes until browned.

7 Add the garlic and cook for 1 minute.

8 Add the escarole and 3 tablespoons of the bean cooking water and cook for 5 to 7 minutes.

9 Add the cannellini beans, red pepper, and salt and black pepper to taste.

10 Spoon a portion of the escarole/bean mixture onto individual serving plates. Place one of two fillets on top and spoon pan juices over it. Serve.

# OSSO BUCO *di* PESCATRICE
## *Monkfish Osso Buco*

Classic *osso buco* is a stewed veal shank served over a bed of rice Milanese. The sinewy shank is slow-cooked for hours until fork tender, the perfect treatment. A few years ago, when monkfish started becoming popular in restaurants, I was studying a fillet in the kitchen when, all of a sudden, the bone jumped out at me—it looked just like the veal shank. I then tried cooking the fish in the same way, with tomatoes and onions and herbs, and it was great. In place of rice, try *fregola*, a Sardinian pasta that is a variation on couscous. A bonus: Instead of taking two hours to simmer the way the veal version does, this *osso buco* cooks in just half an hour on top of the stove. **SERVES 4 TO 6**

2½ pounds monkfish tail, bone in, cut into 4 equal pieces

Salt

Freshly ground black pepper

Flour for dusting

½ cup extra virgin olive oil

5 tablespoons finely chopped fresh Italian parsley

2 teaspoons minced garlic

½ teaspoon crushed red pepper

½ cup diced leek

1 cup diced celery

1 cup diced red onion

½ cup diced carrot

½ cup diced red bell pepper

1 cup diced fennel

1 cup diced zucchini

1 cup canned whole tomatoes, with their juice, crushed (You can also use canned crushed tomatoes, but I think the whole ones are less acidic and of better quality.)

1 cup dry white wine

3 cups fish stock (page 120)

2 cups *fregola* or Israeli couscous (Sources, page 221)

---

**WINE SUGGESTION:** *Have white wine with this monkfish—either a full-bodied Chardonnay, like a Capannelle buttery Chardonnay, or a dry Riesling.*

---

*(continued)*

1  Clean the fish by removing the dark skin around the outside. Tie each piece separately with butcher's twine to hold it together, making a snug loop around the perimeter of the piece. Season the fish with salt and pepper to taste and dust with flour.

2  Coat the bottom of a large skillet with ⅓ cup of the olive oil and heat over medium-high heat. Add the fish, and brown it on the top, bottom and sides for about 2 minutes.

3  Coat the bottom of a separate skillet with 3 tablespoons of the remaining olive oil. Add ¼ cup of the parsley, the garlic, and crushed red pepper and sauté briefly over medium heat. Before the garlic colors, add all of the diced vegetables and sauté for 5 minutes. Season with salt and pepper.

4  Add the fish, tomatoes, and wine. Cover the skillet and simmer for 5 minutes.

5  Add the fish stock and *fregola* to the skillet. Cover and cook for about 10 minutes. (If you're using couscous, remove the skillet from the heat and let stand for about 5 minutes.)

6  To serve, remove the fish pieces and cut off the strings. Sprinkle the remaining 1 tablespoon parsley on top of the plated fish, drizzle each piece with a little olive oil, and serve.

# ORATA in STILE MIO

## Sea Bream, My Way

When I lived in Tuscany, I had a garden I dubbed *l'arometo* because it was full of aromas and planted with every conceivable herb. My mom, a fanatic weeder, spent hours out there, keeping the garden tidy. But when a friend gave me some lemongrass to grow, she didn't realize it was something I was trying to cultivate, since it wasn't a plant she'd ever before seen. Every time I'd plant a new batch, Rosa would pull it up, thinking it was a weed. Whenever I make this *orata*, I think of her hunched over the *arometo*, pulling out the lemongrass stalk by stalk. I especially like cooking sea bream in this simple way because it makes the flavor of the fish the star of the dish. **SERVES 4 TO 6**

4 tablespoons fresh oregano leaves, plus 4 whole sprigs

3 tablespoons fresh marjoram

3 tablespoons chopped fresh Italian parsley

1 teaspoon crushed red pepper

5 teaspoons roughly chopped garlic, plus 4 whole cloves, slightly crushed

4 tablespoons chopped lemongrass (Trim 1 inch from the bottom and discard outer leaves before chopping.)

1 cup extra virgin olive oil, plus more for finishing

Four 1¼-pound cleaned whole sea bream or porgies (or red snapper or sea bass)

8 slices lemon

Salt

Freshly ground black pepper

1 tablespoon lemon juice, for finishing

**WINE SUGGESTION:** *Try whites like Vernaccia, Vermentino or Sauvignon Blanc with this dish — basically wines that have a citrusy flavor.*

1 Combine the oregano leaves, marjoram, parsley, crushed red pepper, chopped garlic, and lemongrass in a food processor and puree. With the processor running, slowly drizzle in the olive oil to make a marinade.

2 Coat the outside and inside cavity of each fish with the marinade. Place the fish in a glass bowl or dish, cover with plastic wrap, and refrigerate for at least 12 hours and up to 48 hours.

3 Preheat the oven to 375° F.

*(continued)*

4 Shake off the excess marinade from each fish and stuff the cavity of each with a crushed garlic clove, a sprig of oregano, and 2 lemon slices. Season with salt and pepper.

5 Arrange the fish in a single layer in an ovenproof dish. Bake, uncovered, for 25 minutes, or until cooked through. (If you are using a single large fish, it will take 7 to 10 minutes longer.)

6 Transfer the fish to individual serving plates, drizzle with the lemon juice and olive oil, and serve.

# BRANZINO *con* CAVOLFIORE
## *Sea Bass with Cauliflower*

Cauliflower seems like such a universal vegetable that it is hard to believe that Italy was just about the only place you could find it until the sixteenth century. National pride aside, I like cauliflower because it's so flexible, like pasta, the perfect accompaniment to just about anything. **SERVES 4**

5 cups mixed cauliflower (romanesco, regular white, and purple), cut into small florets

1 pound Idaho potatoes, peeled and cut into ¼-inch slices (3 cups)

¼ cup extra virgin olive oil, plus more for pan

Salt

Freshly ground black pepper

¼ cup diced red onion

1 tablespoon chopped fresh Italian parsley

½ teaspoon crushed red pepper

1 tablespoon minced garlic

¼ cup canned whole tomatoes, with their juice, crushed (You can also use canned crushed tomatoes, but I think the whole ones are less acidic and of higher quality.)

½ cup dry white wine

Four 7- to 8-ounce sea bass fillets

1 Preheat the broiler.

2 Bring a large pot of salted water to a boil and add the cauliflower. Cook 3 to 5 minutes and drain. Set aside.

WINE SUGGESTION: *The vintner, Elisabetta, just west of the Tuscan coastline, makes Aulo Bianco, a Trebbiano blend that I think works well with this sea bass. Or go with any slightly floral white that you like.*

3 In a bowl toss the potatoes with 2 tablespoons of the olive oil and salt and pepper to taste. Arrange the potatoes on a baking sheet in a single layer and broil for 10 minutes, or until browned on top. Set aside.

4 Preheat the oven to 375° F.

5 Coat the bottom of a large skillet with the remaining 2 tablespoons olive oil. Add the onion, parsley, crushed red pepper, and garlic and sauté over medium heat for 10 to 15 minutes, or until the onion is translucent. Add the tomatoes and their juice. Add the cauliflower and wine and bring to a boil. Reduce to a simmer and cook 2 to 3 minutes. Season with salt and pepper.

6 Oil the bottom of a large casserole and in it make a layer of the potatoes. Spoon three quarters of the cauliflower mixture on top.

7 Season the sea bass fillets with salt and pepper and arrange them in a single layer on top of the vegetables. Layer with the remaining cauliflower mixture. Cover the pan with foil and bake for 12 to 18 minutes, until the fish is cooked through.

8 Serve each fillet with some of the vegetables and spoon pan juices over it.

# BRANZINO con FUNGHI

## Sea Bass with Mushrooms

In the summer, when porcini are in season in Tuscany, mushroom sellers head for the seaside because they know how popular porcini are with tourists eating in restaurants, especially Italian tourists. Along the same lines, restaurants are happy to pay top dollar for the mushrooms so they can put them on their menus. In my book, this is a win-win-win situation, with sellers, restaurants, and diners all happy. Since fresh porcini are hard to find, I use shiitake, cremini, and oyster mushrooms here; if you can find fresh porcini, so much the better. **SERVES 4**

5 tablespoons extra virgin olive oil

3 teaspoons minced garlic

¼ cup chopped fresh Italian parsley

2 teaspoons chopped fresh oregano

½ pound cremini mushrooms, sliced (2½ cups)

½ pound shiitake mushrooms, sliced (2½ cups)

¼ pound sliced oyster mushrooms (2½ cups)

½ cup dry white wine

Salt

Freshly ground black pepper

1 cup canned whole tomatoes, with their juice, pureed (You can use canned pureed tomatoes, but I think the whole ones are less acidic and of higher quality.)

Four 7- to 8-ounce sea bass fillets

---

**WINE SUGGESTION:** *A classic combination here would be a Chardonnay like Le Bruniche from the maker Nozzole, but I also like a light Pinot Nero with this dish.*

---

1 Coat the bottom of a large skillet with 2 tablespoons of the olive oil. Add the garlic and cook over medium heat until it starts to color. Add the parsley and oregano and sauté for 20 to 30 seconds.

2 Add all of the mushrooms and sauté over medium-high heat until they become soft. Add ¼ cup of the wine and reduce by half. Season with salt and pepper to taste. Add the tomatoes and ½ cup water. Cover and simmer for 15 to 20 minutes.

**3** Coat the bottom of another large skillet with the remaining 3 tablespoons olive oil and heat over medium heat. Add the fish fillets and sprinkle them with salt and pepper. Sauté for 1 to 2 minutes on each side, add the remaining ¼ cup wine, and cook for 2 to 3 minutes.

**4** Add the mushroom/tomato mixture to the fish. Taste for seasoning, cover, and simmer over medium heat for 3 to 4 minutes. Plate the fish, spoon the mushroom sauce on top, and serve.

## • IL TALISMANO DELLA FELICITA •

Up until relatively recently, we didn't have much of a cookbook culture in Italy. People basically learned to cook from their moms, or in my case, from my mom and dad. One of the few exceptions is *Il Talismano della Felicita* (*The Talisman of Happiness*), a book written in 1929 that is still in print. It made its author, Ada Boni, famous in the same the way *Joy of Cooking* launched Irma Rombauer.

My mom gave me my copy of *Il Talismano* when I started cooking school in Montecatini. It was the only cookbook she ever bought. I love it to this day mostly because she wanted me to go into medicine or teaching, anything but the family business. Knowing that was just more of an incentive for me, and I poured myself into my cooking classes, studying *Il Talismano* in my spare time as if it were the *Gazzetta dello Sport*. With recipes from all over Italy—forty ways to make risotto alone—it was innovative even thirty years ago.

Like the *Joy of Cooking*, *Il Talismano* is a manual. The writing is straightforward, with none of the over-sized opinions so popular in cookbooks today. The big difference is that Signora Boni assumes her readers know how to cook, so there are hardly any quantities or cooking times, only Italian notations, like q.b. (*quanto basta*—as much as you need). There are other assumptions made, too, notably when a pizza recipe starts off, "Buy the dough from your baker." But you can't beat it as a reference, and if you've got the time, I'd check out Signora Boni's other titles translated into English: *La Cucina Regionale Italiana* (*Regional Cooking of Italy*) and *Il Piccolo Talismano* (*The Little Talisman*), a kind of CliffsNotes version of *Il Talismano*.

# BRANZINO *con* PATATE *e* CARCIOFI

## *Sea Bass with Potatoes and Artichokes*

This recipe is about flexibility Italian style. Though fish and potatoes define the dish, it's the "accent" vegetable that reflects the season. In this version, the accent is artichokes for spring. But you can substitute everything from asparagus to zucchini. What I like about artichokes is how they contrast with the sweetness of the potatoes. Experiment with what you find at your local farmer's market, remembering that the "flexible" vegetable will only be in the oven for about twenty minutes, so it might have to be precooked. In a pinch, you can also use steamed frozen artichoke hearts; they're not quite the same, but an easy substitute. **SERVES 4**

1 lemon

2½ pounds baby artichokes (or substitute globe artichoke hearts and bottoms or frozen artichoke hearts)

1 pound Idaho potatoes, peeled and sliced ⅛ inch thick (3 cups)

4 teaspoons sliced garlic

1 tablespoon chopped fresh rosemary

2 tablespoons thinly sliced fresh basil

4 canned plum tomatoes, drained and cut lengthwise into 6 slices

3 tablespoons extra virgin olive oil

Salt

Freshly ground black pepper

½ cup vegetable stock

Four 7- to 8-ounce wild striped bass fillets

¼ cup dry white wine

**WINE SUGGESTION:** *I like wines with the slightly mineral taste of grapes grown by the sea here. Look for whites from the area of Maremma, like Litorale Vermentino. A Pinot Grigio would be good, too.*

1  Preheat the oven to 400° F.

2  Fill a bowl with water. Cut the lemon in two and squeeze the juice into the water. Add the squeezed lemon halves to the water, too. If you are using baby artichokes, peel the outer leaves from the artichoke until you reach the part where the leaves are mostly a creamy yellow. Cut the top inch off the artichoke and trim away the stem so that you are left with a golf ball-sized heart. Slice into ¼-inch pieces and place in the lemon water. (For globe artichokes, remove the tough outer leaves and cut the artichokes into wedges. Remove the choke and the soft curly leaves above it. Slice and place in the lemon water.) Set aside. Drain before using.

**3** In a large bowl combine the artichokes, potatoes, garlic, rosemary, basil, tomatoes, and salt and pepper to taste. Add the olive oil and toss to coat.

**4** Place the potato mixture in a large ovenproof baking dish, add the vegetable stock, and cover with aluminum foil. Bake for 35 to 45 minutes, or until the potatoes are soft. Spoon out a quarter of the vegetables into a bowl. Reserve.

**5** Season the fish with salt and pepper and rub the fillets with a little olive oil. Arrange the fillets on the potato and artichoke mixture and add the wine. Cover the fish with the reserved potato mixture. Bake, uncovered, for 8 to 10 minutes, or until the fish is cooked through. Serve.

# PESCE ALL' ISOLANA

## *Red Snapper with Potatoes and Tomatoes*

*Isolana* means island style in Italian and you'll find fish prepared this way in places like Elba, the tiny Tuscan island where Napoleon was exiled. I like this dish because it's easy and makes an impressive presentation at the dinner table. I used to cook this with Chilean sea bass, but since it's been fished almost to extinction, I've started using red snapper instead. You can also go with one of the many other types of sea bass, like black sea bass or striped bass. Even grouper would be good here. **SERVES 6**

One 4-pound red snapper, cleaned

Salt

Freshly ground black pepper

2 sprigs fresh rosemary, plus 1 tablespoon finely chopped

4 sprigs fresh sage, plus 1 tablespoon finely chopped

2 whole garlic cloves, plus 2 teaspoons minced

¼ cup extra virgin olive oil, plus more for brushing

2 pounds potatoes, peeled and sliced into ⅛-inch-thick slices (12 cups)

¾ cup canned tomatoes, drained and sliced lengthwise into quarters

20 whole fresh basil leaves

1 cup dry white wine

---

**WINE SUGGESTION:** *With this dish, I like wines made from the Trebbiano grape, especially from the Elban producer, Sapere Vineyards. But since those wines are hard to find in the United States, look for a Sauvignon Blanc, or a light young Cabernet Franc.*

1 Preheat the oven to 375° F.

2 Rinse the fish inside and out, pat dry with paper towels, and season inside and out with salt and pepper to taste. Place 1 sprig rosemary, 2 sprigs sage, and a garlic clove in the cavity. Set aside.

**3** Rub a large ovenproof dish with olive oil. Combine in the dish the potatoes, tomatoes, chopped rosemary, chopped sage, minced garlic, basil leaves, ½ cup of the wine, the olive oil, and salt and pepper. Arrange in an even layer and bake for 20 minutes. Remove the vegetables from the oven, stir in the remaining ½ cup wine, and add 1 cup water if the mixture seems dry.

**4** Place the fish on the vegetables. With a very sharp knife, score the fish in a continuous zigzag pattern from the gills to the tail. Brush with olive oil. Cover the dish with aluminum foil and bake for 25 minutes. Remove the foil, brush the fish with more olive oil, and bake for 5 minutes. Baste with pan juices and bake another 5 minutes. Transfer the fish and vegetables to a platter and serve.

# BACCALÀ *con* PORRI

## *Salted Codfish with Leeks*

Oddly enough, the two places in Tuscany where salted codfish is most popular are both on the sea—Pisa and Livorno. Obviously, they have plenty of fresh fish in those places, but traditions die hard, and the famous codfish *alla Livornese* is centuries old. (It originated with sixteenth-century Basque fishermen.)

When I was growing up, we'd wash the salt out of the cod by leaving it in the village fountain for a day. Today most housewives let it sit under running water in the sink; it's less picaresque, but probably more hygienic. **SERVES 4**

½ pounds baccalà (salted codfish)

¼ cup extra virgin olive oil

1 tablespoon chopped garlic

2 cups sliced leeks (white part only)

½ teaspoon crushed red pepper

1 tablespoon chopped fresh Italian parsley

1 cup dry white wine

1 cup chopped canned tomatoes

8 cups hot Basic Polenta (page 198) or 4 thick slices of toasted Tuscan bread

**WINE SUGGESTION:** *The Ansonica grape, which dates to Etruscan times, is an anchor in Tuscan white wine-making, and is very nice with cod. Most of the time, though, we'd drink a chilled light Chianti with this dish.*

1 Soak the codfish in cold water to cover for 48 hours, changing the water two or three times. Drain.

2 In a large stockpot bring 4 quarts of water to a boil over medium heat. Add the codfish and boil for 20 minutes. Remove the fish from the water and pat dry. Set aside.

3 Coat the bottom of a medium skillet with the olive oil. Add the garlic, leeks, crushed red pepper, and parsley and sauté over medium heat 10 to 15 minutes, or until the leeks soften and start to color.

4 Add the wine and reduce by half. Add the tomatoes and cook 10 minutes.

5 Add the cod to the skillet with 2 to 3 cups water and salt and pepper to taste. Cover and cook for 25 minutes. Serve with hot polenta or over toasted Tuscan bread.

# PALOMBO *con* PISELLI *e* POMODORI

## *Braised Mako Shark with Peas and Tomatoes*

Fish and peas are a natural combination since they're both sweet and mild but, honestly, fresh fish is rare in landlocked towns like Lucca, where I grew up. We ate shark was because it lasts a little longer than most other fish and didn't spoil on its way in from the coast. We ate this dish a lot on Fridays, especially in the spring. Italians sometimes call shark the veal of the sea because the flesh is so white. **SERVES 4 TO 6**

Four 8-ounce Mako shark fillets

Salt

Freshly ground black pepper

Flour for dusting

4 tablespoons extra virgin olive oil

½ cup thinly sliced scallions (white part only)

2 tablespoons chopped fresh Italian parsley

1 teaspoon finely chopped fresh marjoram

1 teaspoon crushed red pepper

1 cup dry white wine

2 cups canned whole tomatoes, with their juice, crushed (You can use crushed canned tomatoes, but I think the whole ones are less acidic and of higher quality.)

3 cups green peas, fresh or frozen

**WINE SUGGESTION:** *Tuscan Merlots have a softness to them you don't find elsewhere. The cooked tomatoes in this recipe are slightly sweet, which goes well with Merlots from around the area of Montalcino, like Castelgiocondo Lamaione from Frescobaldi or Mandrielle from Castello Banfi.*

1 Season the shark with salt and pepper to taste and dust with flour.

2 Coat a large skillet with 3 tablespoons of the olive oil and heat over medium heat. Add the fish and brown, 4 to 5 minutes per side. Remove from the skillet and reserve.

3 Remove any burned bits from the skillet. Add the remaining tablespoon olive oil, the scallions, parsley, marjoram, and crushed red pepper and sauté over medium heat for 3 to 4 minutes.

4 Add the wine and reduce by half.

5 Add the tomatoes and peas to the pan. Season with salt and pepper and cook for 5 minutes.

6 Add the shark and braise for 5 to 7 minutes on each side. Add ¼ cup water if the sauce is too thick. Taste for seasoning and serve.

# TERRACOTTA

## Chicken under a Brick

This dish is normally called *pollo al mattone*, but I call it *terracotta* because of the special terracotta press I use as weights on the chickens. (If you can find these presses, they're worth the investment; they don't cost much and make a spectacular presentation. But you can also use any sort of ovenproof ten-pound weight, from bricks to hand barbells).

This recipe works best when the chicken has been marinated for twenty-four hours before cooking, but you can make the dish on the spur of the moment, too. The ginger and lemongrass, both common ingredients in Roman times, give the chicken a nice kick.

SERVES 3 TO 4

2 teaspoons minced garlic

1½ teaspoons finely chopped fresh thyme

1 teaspoon crushed red pepper

3 tablespoons minced ginger

½ cup minced fresh lemongrass

1 teaspoon finely chopped fresh rosemary

1 teaspoon finely chopped fresh sage

Pinch ground allspice

Pinch grated nutmeg

Pinch ground cloves

½ cup extra virgin olive oil, plus 2 tablespoons for the pan

One 4-pound chicken, split in half, backbone removed

Salt

Freshly ground black pepper

½ cup dry white wine

1 tablespoon lemon juice

WINE SUGGESTION: *I like this dish with a bright, dense Chianti Classico like Lucius from Fattoria Viticcio. The owner named the wine for his father, who died in 1997, the first year of its release. I think the wine lives up to the honor.*

1 To make the marinade: Combine half of the garlic, half of the thyme, half of the crushed red pepper, half of the ginger, all of the lemongrass, all of the rosemary and sage, the allspice, nutmeg, and cloves in a blender or food processor. With the machine running, slowly drizzle in the ½ cup olive oil.

2 Coat the chicken with the marinade, sprinkle with salt and pepper to taste, and cover. Refrigerate at least 12 hours but no more than 48 hours.

3 For the glaze: Combine the white wine, the remaining garlic, thyme, ginger, crushed red pepper, and lemon juice. Reserve.

4 Preheat the oven to 500° F.

5 Coat the bottom of a large ovenproof skillet with the remaining 2 tablespoons olive oil. Use more if there isn't enough to coat the pan. Heat over high heat.

6 Remove the chicken from the marinade and put it skin side down in the hot skillet. Place another ovenproof pan directly on top of the chicken and put a 10-pound weight on top. Bake the chicken for 20 to 25 minutes. Remove the chicken from the oven and discard any excess fat from the pan. At this point the chicken should have a very nice dark brown crust.

7 Remove the weight and pan, turn the chicken over, and pour the glaze into the skillet. Put the second skillet and the weight back on top of the chicken and return the pan to the oven for 20 to 25 minutes. Serve immediately, with the glaze used as a sauce.

# POLLO FRITTO
## *Tuscan Fried Chicken*

Get in line if you think fried chicken originated in the American South. As close as I can figure, fried chicken came to Italy before it came to North America, though Africa was probably the source in both cases. Back when the Romans controlled everything from Sicily to Scotland, territories sent their best foods back to Rome as a tribute. My guess is that some African ruler at the time dispatched a batch—or someone who knew how to cook one up— to be served to the emperor.

I have been eating this dish since I was old enough to say drumstick, but since I put it on the menu at Beppe, probably the single most asked question from diners is why we serve fried chicken. As I've explained a million times, fried dishes are a huge part of Italian home cooking. We fry everything, from brains to apples to veal. A Tuscan proverb: Even old shoes are good if they're fried. My mom used to make this fried chicken for summer picnics or for dinner when friends came over. At Beppe, I toss in handfuls of rosemary, sage, and thyme for a lovely herby scent. **SERVES 4**

Two 3-pound chickens, cut into 8 pieces each

Salt

Freshly ground black pepper

6 tablespoons lemon juice

Peanut or vegetable oil, for frying

3 cups flour

4 eggs, beaten with salt and pepper

6 sprigs fresh thyme

6 sprigs fresh sage

6 sprigs fresh rosemary

6 garlic cloves, peeled flattened with your hand

**WINE SUGGESTION:** *With fried chicken, I like a rosé or a light Chianti. On the other hand, something fuller like Magari, a Merlot blend from the Gaja Ca' Marcanda vineyard in Maremma would also be delicious.*

1 Season the chicken pieces with salt and pepper and 4 tablespoons of the lemon juice. Cover and marinate for 1 hour at room temperature.

2 Fill a frying pan large enough to hold all of the chicken halfway with the peanut or vegetable oil. Heat to 375° F on a deep-fat thermometer.

3 Season the flour with salt and pepper. Dredge the chicken in the flour, then dip it in the beaten eggs. Carefully place the chicken pieces in the hot oil, but don't overcrowd the pan. The temperature of the oil will drop when you add the chicken. Fry the pieces for 15 to 20 minutes at a temperature between 325° and 350°. If all the chicken does not fit in the pan at one time, start with the larger pieces, remove a few when cooked to drain on paper towels, and proceed to fry the smaller pieces.

4 During the last two minutes of cooking time, add the thyme, sage, rosemary, and garlic and fry until crisp.

5 Drain the fried chicken on paper towels. Season with salt and pepper and drizzle with the remaining 2 tablespoons lemon juice. Serve the chicken topped with the fried herbs and garlic.

# CACCIUCCO *di* POLLO

## *Chicken Stew*

In the early 1900s, there was a group of intellectuals who met in a small lakeside cabin in the town of Torre del Lago to discuss everything from current events to music. In honor of their most famous member, the composer Giacomo Puccini, they called themselves Club della Boheme. Often the meetings centered around cooking dinner. This dish was the specialty of Giovanni Gragnani, a founding member of the club, who took the classic idea of a mixed fish stew and substituted chicken for the fish. It's flavorful and tender, and I especially love it on a cold night spooned over thick Tuscan bread to warm me up. **SERVES 4 TO 6**

1 teaspoon ground cumin seed

1 teaspoon crushed red pepper

¼ teaspoon grated nutmeg

4 tablespoons minced garlic

2 teaspoons finely chopped fresh rosemary

1 tablespoon finely chopped fresh sage

2 teaspoons finely chopped fresh thyme

9 tablespoons extra virgin olive oil

Salt

Freshly ground black pepper

Two 3-pound chickens, cut into 8 pieces each

2 cups chicken stock

3 tablespoons lemon juice

1 cup dry white wine

2 cups canned plum tomatoes, with their juice, pureed

2 cups julienned carrots sticks, ½ by 1 inch

4 cups thinly sliced red onions

3½ cups julienned celery sticks, ½ by 1 inch

3 cups julienned fennel

½ pound shiitake, oyster, or cremini mushrooms, sliced thin (4 cups)

3 tablespoons finely chopped Italian parsley

---

**WINE SUGGESTION:** *A full-bodied white would be great with this stew. Look for Gualdo del Re Val di Cornia Eliseo, a blend of Trebbiano, Malvasia, and Clairette grapes.*

---

1 For the marinade: In a bowl large enough to hold all the chicken pieces, mix together the cumin seed, crushed red pepper, nutmeg, 2 teaspoons of the garlic, rosemary, sage, thyme, 6 tablespoons of the olive oil, and salt and pepper to taste. Add the chicken, coat well, and refrigerate at least ½ hour and up to 48 hours.

2 Preheat oven to 375° F.

3 Remove the chicken from the refrigerator and discard the juices that have collected in the bowl. Coat a large casserole with the remaining 3 tablespoons olive oil and arrange the chicken in the dish. Bake for 20 minutes.

4 Add the chicken stock, lemon juice, remaining garlic, and wine and bake for another 20 minutes, or until the liquid has reduced by half.

5 Toss the tomatoes with the carrots, onions, celery, fennel, mushrooms, and parsley. Season with salt and pepper and arrange on top of the chicken. Cover the casserole with aluminum foil and bake for 1 hour, basting occasionally with the pan juices.

6 Remove the chicken pieces from the baking dish and let cool for 5 to 10 minutes. Remove the bones, leaving the meat in large pieces, and return the meat to the casserole. Stir the vegetables and chicken together and adjust the seasonings. Bake 20 minutes. Serve hot.

# BILLO *della* TREBBIATURA
## *Grain Harvest Turkey*

You would be hard-pressed to find turkey on a Tuscan table, except maybe on Christmas or New Year's Eve. (I think the very first time my mom made it was on Thanksgiving at my in-laws in Florida a few years ago.) Still, there are a few recipes for it, like this one, part of a traditional meal served during the grain harvest. A turkey had the dual advantage of being able to feed a lot of people cheaply and was one of the few examples of an Italian one-pot meal—thus freeing women to work in the fields instead of the kitchen. Ask your butcher to prepare the turkey for you in two-inch chunks. **SERVES 8 TO 10**

½ cup extra virgin olive oil

4–5 pounds dark and light turkey meat, cut into 1- by 3-inch chunks

2 ounces pancetta, minced (½ cup)

¾ cup crumbled Italian sausage, half sweet, half hot

4 cups diced onions

2 cups diced carrots

3 cups diced celery

¼ cup minced garlic

Pinch crushed red pepper

1½ tablespoons finely chopped fresh rosemary

1½ tablespoons finely chopped fresh sage

3 tablespoons finely chopped fresh Italian parsley

Salt

Freshly ground black pepper

1 cup dry white wine

8 cups canned whole tomatoes, with their juice, crushed (You can use canned crushed tomatoes, but I think the whole ones are less acidic and of higher quality.)

1 pound rigatoni or penne

1 cup grated Parmesan cheese

---

**WINE SUGGESTION:** *Try the innovative Tenuta di Trinoro red blend, Le Cupole, which is made from four grapes (Cabernet Franc, Cabernet Sauvignon, and Cesanese). Le Cupole is great with stews.*

---

1 Coat the bottom of a large skillet with the olive oil and heat over medium heat. Add the turkey meat, pancetta, and sausage and cook until the meat begins to brown.

2 Add the onions, carrots, celery, garlic, crushed red pepper, rosemary, sage, and 1½ tablespoons of the parsley. Season with salt and pepper to taste and cook for 10 to 15 minutes.

3 Add the wine and simmer until reduced by half.

4 Add the tomatoes to the pan with enough water to cover all the ingredients. Bring to a simmer and cook the sauce for 1½ hours, adding more water if needed.

5 Bring a large pot of well-salted water to a boil. Add the rigatoni and cook until very *al dente*, about 7 to 8 minutes. Drain, reserving 1 cup of the cooking water.

6 Add the pasta to the sauce with ½ cup of the cooking water. Simmer 2 to 3 minutes for the rigatoni to absorb some of the sauce. If the mixture seems dry add a little more pasta cooking water. Adjust the seasonings. Toss and serve sprinkled with the grated Parmesan and the remaining 1½ tablespoons parsley.

# TACCHINO INPORCHETTATO
## con CASTAGNE e PATATE
### Turkey Roasted Pork Style with Chestnuts and Potatoes

As I've said before, it would be rare to find turkey on the menu of a restaurant in Italy. But back when I was living at Vipore, I had a group of American friends who wanted turkey for Thanksgiving, a holiday I'd never heard of. I figured the only way I could meet their request would be to treat the bird as if it were pork. So I butterflied a turkey breast, covered it with filling, and rolled it up like porchetta, a slow-roasted pork tenderloin I'd been making all my life. Later, when I learned Americans put all their turkey stuffing in the cavity, I was impressed with my version: It was a more efficient way of spreading the flavor of the stuffing over all the meat. I liked the result so much I started making it year round. **SERVES 6 TO 8**

1 cup dried chestnuts (or 2 cups fresh)

1 bay leaf

Salt

2 tablespoons finely chopped fresh thyme

3 tablespoons finely chopped fresh rosemary

3 tablespoons finely chopped fresh sage

½ pound pancetta, diced (2½ cups)

3 tablespoons minced garlic

½ cup extra virgin olive oil

One 4- to 5-pound turkey breast

Freshly ground black pepper

¾ cup diced onion

1 cup diced carrot

1 cup diced celery

2½ pounds potatoes, peeled and diced (7 cups)

2 cups dry white wine

2 cups chicken stock (page 66)

---

**WINE SUGGESTION:** *Try Cum Laude, a full-bodied red from the area of Montalcino, one of the newest Super Tuscans. Cum laude is Latin for "with honors" and the wine deserves the name. Another good pick would be a Cabernet Sauvignon, Merlot, and Syrah blend.*

---

1 Preheat the oven to 400° F.

2 Put the dried chestnuts in a small saucepan, fill the pan with water, and add the bay leaf and salt to taste. Bring to a simmer and cook until the chestnuts are soft, 30 to 40 minutes. Drain and reserve. (If you are using fresh chestnuts, preheat the oven to 350° F. Using a sharp knife, cut an X in the shell. Bake the chestnuts on a cookie sheet for 20 to 30 minutes until they open. Let cool, peel, and reserve.)

3 Combine the chopped herbs, pancetta, and garlic in a food processor. With the machine running, drizzle in ¼ cup of the olive oil until the mixture becomes a paste.

4 Butterfly the turkey breast so that it lays flat and pound slightly. Season with salt and pepper to taste. Smear half of the herb/pancetta mixture over the surface. Using your fingers, carefully work your way under the turkey skin to create a big pocket. Spread the remaining pancetta/herb mixture in the pocket. Roll up the turkey. (This will be tricky; you want it to be as tightly rolled as possible.) Tie the turkey securely with butcher's twine.

5 Coat a large roasting pan with the remaining ¼ cup olive oil and spread the onion, carrot, celery, potatoes, and chestnuts evenly over the bottom. Sprinkle with salt and pepper and place the turkey on top. Rub the breast with olive oil and season with salt and pepper. Roast the turkey for 30 minutes.

6 Add the wine to the roasting pan and continue roasting the turkey, basting occasionally, until the bird reaches an internal temperature of 160° F, about 2 to 3 hours. (If you don't have a thermometer, make a small incision and see if the juices run clear. If there is still blood in the juice, the turkey isn't done.) By the end of the cooking time, the skin should be crispy and dark brown. If it starts to get too dark, tent aluminum foil over the breast.

7 Remove the turkey from the pan and let it rest 10 to 20 minutes before slicing. Skim off any excess fat from the pan, add 1 cup water or chicken stock, and bring to a simmer on the stove. Stir the mixture frequently to prevent burning. When the liquid has reduced by half and the potato/chestnut mixture has a stew-like consistency, adjust the seasonings. Transfer the mixture to a serving platter. Remove the twine from the breast and slice the turkey. Serve the slices on top of or next to the potatoes and chestnuts.

# PAPERO *alla* MELARANCIA
## *Orange Roasted Duck*

By the 1300s duck was popular and was being served in Florentine restaurants like Osteria delle Bertucce, a spot believed to be a favorite of the Medici ruler, Lorenzo Il Magnifico.

*Papero alla melarancia* was a natural for the Osteria, since it was located next to gardens stocked with orange trees (which are still there, on Via dei Melaranci, the Renaissance name for oranges). By the time I arrived, some 600 years later, orange duck had disappeared as a Tuscan classic, which seemed a shame, so I tried to revive it. I cooked up my own version at Vipore, my family's restaurant in Tuscany, and have been making it ever since. I love the bitterness of the orange peel with the sweetness of the duck meat. **SERVES 4**

Two 3- to 4-pound ducks

½ pound hot Italian sausage

½ pound sweet Italian sausage

4 ounces pancetta, minced (1 cup)

2 cups diced crustless day-old Italian bread

3 cups diced celery

2 cups diced carrots

10 cups chopped red onions

2 whole garlic cloves, plus 6 sliced

2 tablespoons finely chopped fresh rosemary

2 tablespoons finely chopped fresh sage

1 tablespoon Tuscan Spice (see Sources on page 221), or *garam masala*, or use equal parts of ground allspice, cinnamon, nutmeg, and cloves

1 cup peeled, seeded, and diced orange segments

Salt

Freshly ground black pepper

3 oranges, thinly sliced and seeded, with rind

1½ cups orange juice

½ cup extra virgin olive oil

1 cup chicken or duck stock

1 cup Gran Gala or another orange liqueur

---

**WINE SUGGESTION:** *This rich dish calls for a big wine, like Castelgiocondo Riserva or Brunello di Montalcino Riserva.*

1 Bring a large pot of well-salted water to a boil. Submerge the ducks in the water and cook for 10 minutes. Remove the ducks and let cool. (This step helps render the fat from the duck skin and makes the skin crispy during the roasting process.)

2 Preheat the oven to 375° F.

3 To make the stuffing: Combine both sausages, the pancetta, bread, half of the celery, half of the carrots, 2 cups of the onions, the 2 whole garlic cloves, the rosemary, sage, 2 teaspoons of the Tuscan Spice, the diced oranges, salt and pepper. Add ½ cup of the orange juice and combine well.

4 Wipe out the duck cavities with a paper towel and season with salt and pepper. Divide the stuffing in half and fill each cavity. Secure with a toothpick. Season the outside of the ducks with salt and pepper and sprinkle the remaining Tuscan Spice under the wings.

5 Coat the bottom of a large ovenproof skillet with the olive oil. Add the ducks and roast in the oven for 30 minutes. Remove the skillet from the oven and spoon off the excess fat. Add the remaining celery, carrots, onions, the sliced garlic, and sliced oranges and return the pan to the oven. Roast 20 minutes.

6 Pour ½ cup of the remaining orange juice over the ducks and add the stock and liquor to the pan. Roast for 2 hours, basting every 15 minutes.

7 During the last 15 minutes of roasting, raise the heat to 400° F. This will ensure crispy, caramelized skin.

8 Remove the ducks from the pan and let rest 10 to 15 minutes before carving. Meanwhile, puree the vegetables, 2 or 3 of the orange slices, and the pan juices in a food processor. Transfer the puree to a saucepan and reduce over medium-high heat until thick enough to coat the back of a spoon. Taste for seasonings. Slice the ducks, spoon the puree over the meat, and serve.

# QUAGLIE
## *Grilled Quail*

In Italy, hunters use quail as practice targets, and other than that, you'd have a hard time finding anyone interested in these birds. I felt much the same way until I came to New York and saw quail on so many menus. Curious, I decided to find a supplier and come up with my own interpretation, using some favorite Tuscan ingredients in a decidedly untraditional dish. I went with a light-hearted approach, serving the quail with the pasta, *fregola*, because it looked like bird feed to me, and corn, because that's what quails eat. If you can't find fennel pollen, ground fennel seeds are fine. **SERVES 4**

6 tablespoons extra virgin olive oil

2 ounces pancetta, diced (½ cup)

5 tablespoons roughly chopped fresh sage

5 tablespoons chopped fresh Italian parsley

½ cup fennel fronds

2 tablespoons chopped garlic

2 teaspoons fennel pollen (see headnote) or ground fennel seed

Freshly ground black pepper

4 semi-boneless quail

Salt

2 ears fresh corn, husks intact

1½ cups diced onions

½ pound (1¼ cups) *fregola* (or Israeli couscous, see Sources on page 221)

1 cup roasted red peppers, diced

¼ cup chopped fresh cilantro

---

**WINE SUGGESTION**: *I'd contrast the richness of the quail with a young Sangiovese like Casamatta from the producer Bibi Graetz. Or try a young Merlot.*

---

1 Coat a sauté pan with 3 tablespoons of the olive oil. Add the pancetta and sauté over medium heat for 5 minutes. Set aside.

2 In a food processor chop the sage, 1 tablespoon of the parsley, the fennel fronds, garlic, fennel pollen and pepper to taste. Add the herb mixture to the pancetta and stir well to combine.

3 Wipe out the quail cavities with a paper towel, then stuff them generously with the pancetta mixture. Season the outside of the birds with salt and pepper, then lightly oil the skin with olive oil. Marinate the stuffed birds in the refrigerator for 2 to 24 hours. Let them stand at room temperature for 1 hour before cooking.

4 Preheat the oven to 450° F. or preheat a grill on its highest setting.

5 Peel the husks of the corn back and remove the silk. Cook the corn on the grill or in the oven. On the grill it will take 15 to 20 minutes; in the oven 20 to 30 minutes. When the cobs are cool enough to handle, use a sharp knife to cut off the kernels. There should be about 2 cups. Set aside.

6 Coat the bottom of a large sauté pan with the remaining 3 tablespoons olive oil. Add the onions and sauté over medium heat until they turn golden, 8 to 10 minutes.

7 Add the *fregola* and ½ cup of water. Continue adding water ½ cup at a time, until the *fregola* is *al dente*, about 18 to 20 minutes. Strain the mixture and transfer it to a large bowl. Add the corn kernels, roasted peppers, cilantro, the remaining ¼ cup parsley, and salt and pepper to taste. Set aside.

8 Grill the quail for 7 minutes on each side. Serve with the *fregola* salad.

# CONIGLIO CARI
## *Curried Rabbit*

It is hard to believe that this is a typical dish of Garfagnana, the small hilltop area where my mom grew up, but back in the eighteenth century, when the English started summering in Garfagnana, they brought curry makings with them from home so they could cook up all their favorite dishes on vacation. Many of them ended up giving local residents gifts of curry powder or spices like cumin and cardamom, and slowly the flavor seeped into the cuisine. In the hill towns, they call the spice *cari*, which is as close to pronouncing the word curry as the locals can get. **SERVES 4 TO 6**

1½ cups coarsely chopped onions

3 cups coarsely chopped celery

½ cup coarsely chopped carrots, plus 2 cups sliced carrots

1 tablespoon roughly chopped garlic

2 tablespoons chopped fresh Italian parsley

1 tablespoon chopped fresh rosemary

2 ounces cubed pancetta (½ cup)

3 tablespoons extra virgin olive oil

2 rabbits (2½–3 pounds each), cut into 16 pieces total (ask the butcher to do this)

Salt

Freshly ground black pepper

Pinch crushed red pepper

1 cup dry white wine

1 tablespoon curry powder

3 cups peeled potato chunks

1 bay leaf

---

**WINE SUGGESTION:** *With this spicy rabbit dish, I'd drink a Syrah or Petite Syrah. Or go with something more complex, like SummuS, the Sangiovese/Cabernet Sauvignon/Syrah blend from Castello Banfi.*

---

1  Preheat the oven to 400° F.

2  In a food processor puree the onions, celery, chopped carrots, garlic, parsley, rosemary, and pancetta to a coarse paste. Set aside.

3  Coat the bottom of a large ovenproof skillet with the olive oil and heat over medium heat. Season the rabbit pieces with salt and pepper to taste and arrange them in the skillet. Brown on all sides. Remove the rabbit from the skillet and set aside.

4  Add the pureed vegetable mixture, salt and pepper, and the crushed red pepper to the skillet and sauté over medium for 10 to 15 minutes.

5   Add the wine, curry powder, sliced carrots, potatoes, and rabbit to the skillet. Reduce the wine by half, then add the bay leaf and enough water to come halfway up the rabbit.

6   Transfer the skillet to the oven and bake for 20 minutes. Using tongs, turn the rabbit pieces over and cook another 25 minutes, adding water if the mixture seems dry. Turn the rabbit pieces over again and add more water if needed. Cook 20 minutes.

7   Remove the rabbit pieces from the skillet and keep them warm. Place the skillet on the stovetop. Add enough water to the potato/carrot mixture to create a stew-like consistency and taste for seasonings. Transfer the rabbit to serving plates, spoon the sauce on top, and serve.

## • PELLEGRINO ARTUSI •

Pellegrino Artusi had his moment of fame in the United States a few years ago when Random House published his cookbook *The Art of Eating Well*. It's too bad that was the end of it, because he was such a colorful character, one of the few gourmands to have a role in national affairs.

First, a quick civics lesson. Until 1871, Italy was a group of nation-states that didn't always see eye to eye, and in the early years after unification northerners were still a little wary of southerners, and vice versa. That's where Artusi, a former silk merchant, came in. Artusi's main passion was food, and he decided to write *The Art of Eating Well*, collecting his favorite recipes from every corner of Italy. When the book came out in 1891, it was hardly an instant success—Artusi had to publish it himself—but today the book is considered a landmark since it was the first time that Italy was written about as a unified country.

I'm not so into politics, but what I like about Artusi is how his outsized opinions compare to some of the tea parlor polite food writing of today. Artusi dismisses roasts cooked on the spit if they're stuck with rosemary, garlic, or other herbs. (Such bias would put me out of business, by the way.) He criticizes the Tuscans for using too many vegetables, for throwing away frog eggs, and for even favoring pasta dough that's too thin. A sentence like "Many who read this will think, 'What a ridiculous dish!'" is pretty standard, and his commentary can be as honest as "This is not a dish to go wild over."

# CONIGLIO *con* OLIVE
## *Stewed Rabbit with Olives*

In Italy, this is the dish your fiancé's parents serve the first time you go to meet them. And the big question you hear young people ribbing each other with is directly related: "When are you going to eat rabbit and olives?" Though some Americans thinks the pits in olives are a menace, I like them in this recipe because they add more flavor. You can choose whichever approach you like best. Serve the stew over polenta, or, if you bone the rabbit, over pasta as a sauce. **SERVES 4**

½ ounce dried porcini mushrooms (½ cup)

3–5 tablespoons extra virgin olive oil

Two 2½- to 3-pound rabbits, cut into a total of 16 pieces (ask your butcher to do this)

Salt

Freshly ground black pepper

Flour for dusting

½ cup finely chopped carrot

1 cup finely chopped celery

1 cup finely chopped red onions

2 teaspoons finely chopped garlic

½ teaspoons crushed red pepper

1 sprig fresh sage

1 sprig fresh rosemary

1 tablespoon lemon juice

1 cup dry white wine

1½ cups canned whole tomatoes, with their juice, pureed (You can use canned pureed tomatoes, but I think the whole tomatoes are less acidic and of higher quality.)

1 cup chicken or vegetable stock

1 cup black olives with pits

8 cups hot Basic Polenta (page 198)

---

**WINE SUGGESTION:** *Something with dark berry flavors, like Cabernet Sauvignon would be perfect here. Or, for a real treat, try Do (as in do re mi. The owner is a music fanatic). Do is made from Sangiovese grapes from the Montalcino area and a half dozen other varietals from the Maremma.*

---

1 Soak the porcini in 3 cups warm water to cover for ½ hour. Using your hand, scoop the porcini out of the water, trying not to disturb the sediment on the bottom. Coarsely chop the porcini and set aside. Gently pour two-thirds of the porcini water into another container and reserve. Discard the remaining water.

2 Coat the bottom of a large skillet with 3 tablespoons of the olive oil and heat over medium-high heat. Season the rabbit pieces with salt and pepper to taste and dredge in the flour, shaking off any excess. Put the rabbit in the skillet and brown on all sides. Remove and reserve.

3 Add more olive oil to the skillet if needed. Add the carrot, celery, onions, garlic, crushed red pepper, and sage and rosemary sprigs. Sauté for 10 to 15 minutes, or until the vegetables are soft. Add the lemon juice.

4 Add the wine and scrape any bits of fat or meat stuck to the bottom of the skillet. Reduce the wine by half. Return the rabbit to the skillet.

5 Add the tomatoes, porcini, stock, porcini water, and olives to the skillet. Season with salt and pepper. Bring to a simmer, cover, and cook for 1 hour, occasionally spooning the pan liquids over the meat to keep it moist. Taste for seasonings and serve the rabbit and pan juices over the hot polenta.

# BISTECCA *alla* FIORENTINA

## *Florentine Beefsteak*

Almost everyone now has heard of beefsteak Florentine, but if you'd asked an Italian about it a hundred years ago you would have gotten a puzzled look. For most families, cattle were equal to tractors; it was only after World War II, when the economy took off, that people could really afford steak. Today purists insist the meat come from a Chianina steer, a breed that dates back to Roman times, though it's harder and harder to find such cuts in Italy, and almost impossible in the United States.

About three years ago, I became so obsessed with producing the perfect Fiorentina that I actually started a small Chianina herd here, moving them from Texas to a small farm in upstate New York. They're just beautiful animals, almost as big as oxen, and they produce the best steaks you can imagine. The key to cooking this dish is the level of heat that caramelizes the exterior of the steak, resulting in a memorable crust. **SERVES 4 TO 6**

Four 24-ounce bone-in rib-eye steaks

2 tablespoons sea salt (if using kosher salt, use ½ cup)

1 teaspoon Tuscan Spice (see Sources on page 221), or *garam marsala*, or mix together equal parts of ground allspice, cinnamon, nutmeg, and cloves

1 tablespoon freshly ground black pepper

2–4 tablespoons extra virgin olive oil

---

**WINE SUGGESTION:** *This is probably one of the most famous and traditional dishes from Tuscany. Serve it with a really fine, full-bodied red, like Costanti Brunello di Montalcino. If you want something more affordable, a good Chianti or Rosso di Montalcino would work well, too.*

---

1 Preheat the grill to its highest setting. Or, preheat the broiler.

2 Combine the salt, Tuscan Spice, and pepper, mixing well, and sprinkle half of the mixture onto one side of the steaks.

3 Brush the grill with some of the olive oil. Place the steaks, seasoned side down, on the grill and cook for 4 minutes, until a dark brown crust forms. Season the steaks with the remaining spice mixture, flip the steaks, and grill for 4 to 5 minutes for medium-rare. (It will take less time if the steaks are less than 1 inch thick.) Remove the meat from the grill. (If broiling, follow the same instructions, but start the steaks seasoned side up. Broiling may take longer, depending upon the heat of the broiler.) Let the steaks rest for a few minutes before serving.

# HAMMIN *alla* TOSCANA
## *Tuscan Meat Loaf*

Most of the old Jewish recipes that made their way into the Italian diet are vegetarian, like the famous Roman fried artichokes or Russian salad you find in our version of a deli. Still, there are a few meat dishes we owe to the Jews, the classic being *hammin*, a one-course Sabbath meal that's now common all over Tuscany. (The word *hammim* comes from the Hebrew adjective ham, or warm, which describes certain dishes that were kept warm for prolonged periods of time. In this case it was a way to deal with the restriction of lighting a fire on the Sabbath. A *hammim* dish was put on the heat before the Sabbath started.)

With ingredients like pancetta and Parmesan cheese in it, Italians have obviously put their own spin on the dish. You can also make this recipe as a loaf, but the way we do it in Italy is complicated: We roast it in a pan, turning and basting it like a regular roast, so I prefer the patties option. If you want to try this in a loaf pan, bake the beans separately and spoon them on top. As to why the ratio of beans to meat seems disproportionate, it is because meat was always a precious commodity and used very sparingly. You can reduce the bean serving, but I prefer it like this. **SERVES 4 TO 6**

5 tablespoons extra virgin olive oil

1 cup minced red onions

1 teaspoon minced garlic

1 teaspoon crushed red pepper

1½ pounds ground beef

2 eggs

2 ounces minced pancetta or prosciutto (½ cup)

2 tablespoons grated Parmesan cheese

2 tablespoons Bread Crumbs (page 27)

2 tablespoons chopped fresh Italian parsley

1 teaspoon chopped fresh thyme

Salt

½ cup dry white wine

1 cup chicken or beef stock

7 cups Stewed Beans (page 189)

**WINE SUGGESTION:** *Sometimes with a really simple dish such as this I want a complex wine. Desiderio, which is 100 percent Merlot, is just that—soft and plumy.*

1 Preheat the oven to 375° F.

2 Coat the bottom of a large ovenproof skillet with 2 tablespoons of the olive oil. Add the onions, garlic, and crushed red pepper and sauté over medium heat until the onions start to soften and brown, 10 to 15 minutes. Cool and transfer to a large bowl.

3 Add the beef, eggs, pancetta, Parmesan, bread crumbs, parsley, thyme, and salt to the bowl. Combine well and form into 15 small patties, each about 2½ inches in diameter.

4 Add the remaining 3 tablespoons olive oil to the skillet and heat over medium heat. Add the patties and brown 4 to 5 minutes per side.

5 Drain the fat from the pan. Add the wine and cook until reduced by half. Add the stock and *fagioli all'uccelletto*. Cover the skillet, transfer it to the oven, and bake for 20 minutes. Serve.

# FRANCESINA

## *Sausage and Potato Stew*

When the French navy was stationed in Livorno in the 1800s, its sailors had a reputation with the locals for being stingy. The French also wore hats with red pom-poms. What is the connection to Francesina? Well, the Francesina is the quintessential bargain dinner: The old-fashioned way was to mix meat left over from making broth and potatoes (I use sausage because it's more practical). The tomatoes got tossed in because they were about the same size as the pom-poms the French wore on their hats. A big bowl of Francesina was one of my favorite foods as a kid. Etymology aside, I loved the spark of acidity from the tomatoes and the way the potatoes soaked up the sausage juices. **SERVES 6**

3 tablespoons extra virgin olive oil

1 tablespoon minced garlic

3 whole fresh sage leaves

½ teaspoon crushed red pepper

4 cups celery chunks

1 cup carrot chunks

2 cups red onion chunks

Salt

Freshly ground black pepper

1 pound Italian sausage, cut into ½-inch slices, still in casing; half sweet, half hot

¼ cup dry white wine

2 cups whole canned tomatoes, chopped, with their juice (You can use canned chopped tomatoes, but I think the whole ones are less acidic and of higher quality.)

2 pounds Idaho potatoes, peeled and cut into 2-inch chunks (6 cups)

**WINE SUGGESTION**: *I've tried this dish with just about every wine there is, and the best pairing by far was with a Cabernet Sauvignon. One of my personal favorites, because it is so full, is Farnito from Carpineto.*

1 Coat the bottom of a stockpot with the olive oil. Add the garlic, sage, and crushed red pepper and sauté over medium heat until the garlic begins to color. Add the celery, carrots, and onions. Season with salt and pepper to taste and sauté the vegetables until they begin to soften, 10 to 15 minutes.

2 Add the sausage and cook for 8 to 10 minutes.

3 Add the wine and reduce by half.

4 Add the tomatoes, potatoes, and 2 cups water. Season with salt and pepper. Simmer the stew for 1½ to 2 hours, stirring occasionally and adding more water if the mixture becomes too thick. The Francesina is done when the potatoes are very soft and falling apart. Spoon the stew into bowls and serve.

# MAREMMANA

## *Tuscan Spareribs*

I received lots of good reviews when Beppe opened, but I only saved one, where the critic poked fun at me for serving inauthentic Tuscan food. I laugh now, but at the time it drove me crazy, especially her "proof" that there's no fish in Tuscany and no cowboys who'd eat my "Tuscan spareribs." Putting aside our miles of coastline and towns like Forte di Marmi and Viareggio (she'd obviously never left her hotel when she visited Florence), it was the cowboy reference that got me the most worked up. Granted, Americans might think of cowboys as beef—not pork—eaters. But we not only have cowboys in the Maremma—the famous *butteri*—when Buffalo Bill competed against them in a traveling rodeo show, he lost.

Of course, you won't find a recipe for ribs this way in any Italian cookbook. They are, however, quintessentially Tuscan for me, braised *alla cacciatora*, or hunter's style, in a spicy tomato sauce. You also won't find broccoli rabe in Tuscany, but that's what I serve with my "inauthentic" ribs, because I like the way it compliments the smoky spiciness of the meat. This is definitely a plan-ahead dish. The spareribs need to marinate with the dry rub overnight. Plus I think they taste better if you cook them a day or two in advance and keep them in the refrigerator until the time you want to serve them. **SERVES 6**

¼ cup minced garlic, plus 2 cloves sliced

¼ cup finely chopped fresh sage leaves

¼ cup finely chopped fresh rosemary

2 tablespoons salt

1 tablespoon freshly ground black pepper

1 tablespoon plus 2 teaspoons crushed red pepper

7 pounds pork spareribs

7 tablespoons extra virgin olive oil

3½ cups canned whole tomatoes, crushed (You can use canned crushed tomatoes, but I think the whole ones are less acidic and of higher quality.)

1½ tablespoons Worcestershire sauce

1½ tablespoons hot pepper sauce (like Tabasco)

1 cup dry white wine

---

**WINE SUGGESTION:** *A pure Merlot is perfect here, but if you want to go bigger, try one of the Super-Tuscans like Masseto, a Merlot from Maremma that's reached cult status in the last few years.*

1  For the ribs: Combine the minced garlic, sage, rosemary, salt, black pepper, and 1 tablespoon crushed red pepper. Rub the spareribs well with this mixture and let them marinate, wrapped in plastic, at least 24 hours or up to 48 hours, in the refrigerator.

2  Preheat the oven to 375° F.

3  Coat a large baking pan with ¼ cup of the olive oil and lay the ribs in the pan. Roast stirring, every 20 minutes. After an hour, turn the ribs over and roast 1 hour more. Check the ribs periodically; if the bottom of the pan starts to burn, add a little water.

4  For the tomato sauce: Coat a large skillet with the remaining 3 tablespoons olive oil. Add the sliced garlic and remaining 2 teaspoons crushed red pepper and sauté over medium heat until the garlic begins to color. Add the tomatoes, Worcestershire sauce, and pepper sauce. Add 1½ cups water and bring the tomato sauce to a simmer. Cook for 30 minutes. Taste for seasoning and set aside.

5  When the ribs have browned on both sides, remove them from the pan and drain off any excess fat. Return the ribs to the pan, adding the wine and the tomato sauce. Cover the pan with foil and braise the ribs for 40 minutes. Remove the foil and roast an additional 20 minutes. Serve immediately.

# MILANESE *di* MAIALE
## *Pork Chop Milanese*

I was in Texas recently and laughed when I saw chicken-fried pork chop on the menu. It sounded so southern American but was, in fact, exactly the same as the classic Milanese pork chop, which is pounded super-thin, big as a dinner plate, then breaded, fried, and topped with arugula. In Milan, people call this *cotoletta*, a variation on the Italian word for rib, because in the old days, people used the bone like a handle to eat the pork chop. If you want to be more of a purist, you can leave off all the fancy additions like tomatoes, mushrooms, and truffles in the salad, but I think they add good texture and flavor. **SERVES 4**

½ pound cremini mushrooms

2 teaspoons finely chopped fresh oregano

2 teaspoons finely chopped fresh marjoram

2 plum tomatoes, seeded and sliced lengthwise

¼ cup lemon juice

¼ cup extra virgin olive oil

Salt

Freshly ground black pepper

Four 10-ounce bone-in pork chops, butterflied and pounded ¼ inch thick

1 cup all-purpose flour

Eggwash: 3 eggs beaten with ¼ cup whole milk

2 cups Bread Crumbs (page 27)

Canola or peanut oil, for frying

1 bread slice

2 cups loosely packed arugula or lettuce mixture

1 fresh black truffle (optional)

---

**WINE SUGGESTION:** *A sturdy red is what you need with this pork dish. I am partial to Siepi, a Sangiovese and Merlot blend that's produced in a vineyard more than 800 feet above sea level.*

---

1 Clean the mushrooms with a damp paper towel and cut off the tip of the stems. Slice the mushrooms very thin and put in a bowl. Add the herbs, tomatoes, lemon juice, and olive oil. Season with salt and pepper to taste. Set the salad aside.

2 Sprinkle each pork chop on both sides with salt and pepper. Dredge in flour, shaking off the excess. Dip each chop into the eggwash, letting any excess drip off, then dredge in the bread crumbs.

3 Pour enough canola or peanut oil into a large skillet to measure ½ inch. Heat the oil over medium-high heat until hot. (To test the temperature, drop a piece of bread into the oil. When it sizzles, remove it—the oil is hot enough to use.) Lay the pork chops in the pan one at a time and cook until golden brown and crispy, about 2½ minutes per side. Drain on paper towels.

4 Add the arugula or mixed lettuce to the mushroom salad and toss. Arrange each pork chop on a dinner plate and top with a generous helping of the salad. If using, shave the truffle into thin slices. Scatter the truffle slices over each plate and serve.

# BUGLIONE

## *Lamb Pot Pie*

This dish comes from the Maremma, a coastal area of Tuscany that historically was famous for its wild horses, but today is best known as an emerging wine center. There used to be a lot of coal in the area, too, and when miners would camp out in the woods, they'd throw everything and anything they could find into the campfire stew, from vegetables to mutton bought from a shepherd. They would have sopped it all up with a thick slice of bread, but I decided to top it off with a pie crust to seal in the flavors. The dish is a little like an Italian shepherd's pie, minus the mashed potatoes. I prefer mutton in this stew, but since it can be very hard to find, use lamb instead. **SERVES** 8

¼ cup extra virgin olive oil, plus 1 tablespoon for brushing

Salt

Freshly ground black pepper

Flour for dusting

3 pounds lamb, cut into 1½-inch cubes from the leg

8 cups diced celery

4 cups diced carrots

5 cups diced onions

2 cups diced fennel

3 tablespoons minced garlic

1½ cups dry red wine

2 pounds potatoes, peeled and diced (6 cups)

3 bay leaves

2 cups peas, fresh or frozen

3 cups sliced asparagus (½-inch pieces)

2 tablespoons finely chopped fresh rosemary

2 tablespoons finely chopped fresh thyme

2 tablespoons finely chopped fresh Italian parsley

1¼ pounds focaccia dough (page 44)

Eggwash: 1 egg beaten with 1 tablespoon water

**WINE SUGGESTION:** *I like a strong, peppery red with this pie, like Castello di Fonterutoli, a Chianti from the producer Mazzei. Or go with any Chianti made from 100 percent Sangiovese grapes.*

1 Coat the bottom of a stockpot with the ¼ cup olive oil and heat over medium-high heat. Season the flour with salt and pepper and use dust the lamb cubes. Add the lamb to the pot and brown well on all sides, stirring frequently to prevent sticking. This should take 8 to 10 minutes.

2 Add the celery, carrots, onions, fennel, and 2 tablespoons of the garlic. Cook until the vegetables start to soften, 10 to 15 minutes.

3 Add the wine and reduce by half.

4 Add enough water to just cover the lamb. Add the potatoes and bay leaves and season with salt and pepper to taste. Simmer, uncovered, for 1 hour, stirring frequently to prevent sticking and burning. Add more water if needed.

5 Add the peas, asparagus, the remaining 1 tablespoon garlic, and the fresh herbs. Stir well and simmer for 40 minutes. Taste for seasonings. The stew should be thick and flavorful.

6 Preheat the oven to 475° F.

7 Divide the stew among 8 ovenproof bowls.

8 Divide the focaccia dough into 8 equal balls. Roll each ball into a disk large enough to cover each bowl, with some overhang.

9 Brush the sides of each bowl with the eggwash. Mold a disk over the top of each bowl, being sure to bring it down the sides so it is well anchored. Press the dough onto the side of each bowl to prevent it from coming loose during baking. Brush the dough on each pot pie with olive oil, and sprinkle with salt and pepper. Bake for 20 minutes. When done, the crust should be golden brown and very firm. Serve immediately.

# CONTORNI
## *Vegetables, Beans, and Other Side Dishes*

A *contorno* is, literally, a dish that shapes or gives contours to an entree—an extra. But back in Etruscan times, vegetables were the entrees. In fact, they were almost everything, not because the Etruscans didn't like meat, but because animals were used to plow fields and provide wool. One exception was the pig, which had no domestic chores, and so got sacrificed to the gods as a roast.

What I find amazing is how limited the vegetables choices were back then. Imagine a diet mostly of beets, chicory, garlic, onions, lettuce, peas, cucumbers, and broad beans. Don't get me wrong, I couldn't live without garlic and onions, but I always forget that many of the vegetables we now take for granted were discovered and introduced over time, like potatoes, zucchini, and broccoli. Even tomatoes, technically a fruit, didn't arrive in Italy until the 1500s, when the Jews were driven out of Spain and headed for Livorno.

Since coming to New York, I've adopted the American style of serving the *contorni* on the plate with the entree. That's what my customers like, and, as a chef, it's interesting to think about the tastes that will meld together and complement each other. Discover the *contorni* you like best and pile them on at dinnertime. I have provided wine suggestions for almost all of the recipes in the book so far, but because you don't usually order a wine based on a vegetable side dish, I'm omitting them in this chapter unless the dish could double as an antipasto.

# FUNGHI MISTI TRIFOLATI
## *Sautéed Wild Mushrooms*

For Tuscans, mushroom means porcini, and even today half the fun of eating porcini is foraging for them yourself. It's a little dangerous, of course, since not everyone knows how to recognize porcini from poisonous impostors. The Roman emperor Claudius died in agony after eating a toxic batch; just in case foragers got it wrong, many old recipes even included antidotes. I like preparing porcini in the simplest ways possible: grilled or tossed with Boston lettuce and Parmesan. In this recipe I call for mixed mushrooms because porcini can be hard to find, but if you get fresh porcini, by all means, use them. You can serve this as a side dish for grilled meats, over crostini as an appetizer, or as a pasta sauce. **SERVES 6**

¼ cup extra virgin olive oil

2 tablespoons minced garlic

2 teaspoons chopped fresh oregano

2 teaspoons chopped fresh marjoram

2 tablespoons chopped fresh Italian parsley

½ pound cremini mushrooms, cleaned, stems trimmed, and cut into ¼-inch slices (2½ cups)

¼ pound oyster mushrooms, stems removed and cut into ¼-inch slices (2½ cups)

½ pound shiitake mushrooms, stems removed and cut into ¼-inch slices (2½ cups)

Salt

Freshly ground black pepper

1 cup canned whole tomatoes, with their juice, crushed (You can also use crushed canned tomatoes, but I think the whole ones are less acidic and of higher quality.)

½ cup dry white wine

---

**WINE SUGGESTION:** *If you serve this as an antipasto, pair it with Lucente, a new red wine from the Robert Mondavi-Frescobaldi family collaboration. Lucente's made from Sangiovese, Merlot, and Cabernet Sauvignon grapes and has a nice spiciness to it.*

---

1  Coat the bottom of a large skillet with the olive oil. Add the garlic and chopped fresh herbs and sauté over medium heat until the garlic starts to brown.

2  Raise the heat to high, add all of the mushrooms, and season well with salt and pepper. The mushrooms will release moisture, but if they seem dry add up to ½ cup water. Sauté until softened, 5 to 10 minutes.

3  Remove the mushrooms from the skillet to a bowl. Add the tomatoes and wine to the skillet and simmer for 10 minutes. Return the mushrooms to the pan and cook an additional 5 minutes. Taste for seasonings and serve.

# PATATE *alla* LUCCHESE
## *Roasted Potatoes Lucca Style*

When I was still working in my family's restaurant, Vipore, this is how I roasted potatoes to serve with porchetta. They'd sit on top of an oven after being cooked, so they were always just warm, and I'd steal a few nuggets every time I passed by. **SERVES 6**

2 pounds new potatoes, peeled and sliced ¼ inch thick (6 cups)

3 cups julienned fennel, fronds included (about 1½ pounds)

1½ cups thinly sliced shallots or red onions

5 garlic cloves, unpeeled and crushed

2 sprigs fresh rosemary

3 sprigs fresh sage

½ cup dry white wine

½ cup extra virgin olive oil

Salt

Freshly ground black pepper

1  Preheat the oven to 375° F.

2  Combine all of the ingredients in a large mixing bowl and toss well.

3  Spread the mixture in a single layer in a baking dish. Cover with foil and bake for 25 minutes.

4  With the bottom of a pot or skillet, lightly crush the potatoes to break them up and flatten them slightly. Stir to combine.

5  Return the potatoes to the oven and bake for 20 minutes. When done, the potatoes should be golden brown and crispy on the outside and light and fluffy on the inside. Serve, leaving the garlic cloves in for eaters who like peeling them and spreading the roasted garlic on bread.

# CONCICLA a la COMMODUS

## Green Pea Terrine

This recipe comes from Apicius, the Roman cookbook author. The first time I made it, I barely got a bite, since my wife devoured the entire batch. I've since learned to make a double recipe when we're eating together. **SERVES 6**

2 tablespoons butter, for greasing ramekins

1 cup grated Parmesan cheese

2 tablespoons extra virgin olive oil

1½ cups finely chopped onions

1 tablespoon minced garlic

Pinch crushed red pepper

½ pound bacon or pancetta, finely diced (2 cups)

3⅓ cups green peas, fresh or frozen

2 teaspoons finely chopped fresh marjoram

1 teaspoon finely chopped fresh mint

Salt

Freshly ground black pepper

½ cup dry white wine

2 tablespoons honey

5 eggs, separated

1 tablespoon flour

---

**WINE SUGGESTION:** *If you serve this as an antipasto, pair it with one of my favorites, Brania del Cancello, a Trebbiano and Chardonnay blend from Lucca.*

---

1 Preheat the oven to 325° F.

2 Butter six 4-ounce ovenproof ramekins and dust with ¼ cup of the Parmesan.

3 Coat the bottom of a medium skillet with the olive oil. Add the onions, garlic, crushed red pepper, and bacon and sauté over medium heat until the bacon starts to brown, about 10 minutes.

4 Add the peas, marjoram, and mint. Season with salt and pepper to taste and cook for 12 to 15 minutes.

5 Add the wine and honey. Cook until the wine has reduced, 8 to 10 minutes.

*(continued)*

6　When the wine has evaporated, remove a third of the pea mixture and pulse it to a coarse paste in a food processor. Add the egg yolks and the remaining ¾ cup Parmesan and pulse until they are incorporated. Add the flour and pulse again until just incorporated. Transfer to a large bowl and stir in the reserved peas. Set aside.

7　Put the egg whites in the bowl of an electric mixer. Add a pinch of salt and beat at medium to high speed until they form medium peaks. Fold the whites into the pea mixture a third at a time.

8　Fill each of the prepared ramekins to the top with the pea mixture. Place the ramekins in a roasting pan and pour in water to reach halfway up the sides. Put the pan in the oven and bake for 18 to 20 minutes. The pea mixture should be dark brown on top and slightly puffy. A toothpick should come out clean when inserted in the center of a ramekin. Serve immediately in the ramekins.

# FRISSOGLIA
## Stewed Summer Vegetables

This is a stewed mixed vegetable dish, with an emphasis on zucchini. At Vipore, it was a staple at the beginning of the summer when the gardens were full of asparagus and green beans and zucchini. With the zucchini flowers thrown into the mix, it was lovely to look at, too. You might say *frissoglia* is a little like French *ratatouille*, or if your sympathies are Italian, you might think *ratatouille* is a little like *frissoglia*. **SERVES 6 TO 8**

¼ cup extra virgin olive oil

1 tablespoon sliced garlic

½ teaspoon crushed red pepper

1 cup sliced scallions (both green and white parts)

2 cups sliced green beans (1-inch lengths)

2 cups sliced asparagus (1-inch lengths, keep tips separate)

1 pound Swiss chard, washed, stems cut into 1-inch lengths, and leaves chopped (8 cups)

Salt

Freshly ground black pepper

3 pounds tomatoes, seeded and diced (6 cups)

1½ pounds zucchini, sliced into 1-inch lengths (3 cups)

Zucchini flowers, if available

¼ cup torn fresh basil leaves

2 teaspoons finely chopped fresh marjoram

2 tablespoons grated Parmesan cheese, for finishing

1 Coat the bottom of a stockpot with 2 tablespoons of the olive oil. Add the garlic and crushed red pepper and sauté over medium heat until the garlic begins to color.

2 Add the scallions, green beans, asparagus stems (not the tips), and Swiss chard stems. Season with salt and pepper to taste. Cook the vegetables, stirring occasionally, until all of the liquid they give off evaporates, about 10 minutes.

3 Add the asparagus tips, tomatoes, zucchini, basil, and marjoram and cook until the zucchini starts to soften, about 10 minutes.

4 Add the Swiss chard leaves and season with salt and pepper. Cover and cook for 10 minutes. Add the zucchini flowers and cook 3 minutes more. Taste for seasonings. Drizzle with the remaining 2 tablespoons olive oil and the Parmesan and serve.

# SPINACI SALTATI

## *Sautéed Spinach*

If you use baby spinach, you can add it directly to the oil without cooking it. **SERVES 4 TO 6**

4 pounds spinach, well washed and
tough stems removed

6 tablespoons extra virgin olive oil

3 tablespoons sliced garlic

Salt

Freshly ground black pepper

1 Place the spinach with the water still clinging to the leaves in a pot large enough to hold it. Cover and cook over medium heat, stirring occasionally, until the leaves just wilt, 7 to 8 minutes. Drain well in a colander, pressing out the excess water with the back of a spoon.

2 Coat the bottom of a medium skillet with the olive oil. Add the garlic and sauté until it begins to color, about 5 minutes. Add the spinach and sauté briefly, about 2 minutes. Add salt and pepper to taste and serve.

# FAGIOLI
## *Basic Beans*

You can either soak the beans overnight or use the quick-cook method. There are instructions below for both ways. If you want to freeze some of the beans, remove the quantity to be frozen at a point when they've softened a bit, but are still quite crunchy—that could be anywhere from twenty minutes to an hour of cooking time, depending on the freshness and type of beans. Place the beans in a plastic container and cover them completely with cooking water. Let the beans cool and place them in the freezer. They will keep for up to a month. When you are ready to use the beans, defrost them, add some extra cooking water and cook until soft to the bite. **YIELD: 7 CUPS COOKED**

1 pound (2 ½ cups) cannellini or any other type of dried beans

2 sprigs fresh sage

2 sprigs fresh rosemary

1 head garlic

1 carrot

1 stalk celery

1 onion, quartered

1 tablespoon salt

Extra virgin olive oil, for serving

**LONG-SOAK METHOD:**

1  Pick over the beans to remove any stones or bad or broken beans. Rinse thoroughly.

2  Put the beans in a stockpot and cover with plenty of cold water. Soak for 6 to 12 hours. (If it's warm, put the beans in the refrigerator.)

3  Drain the beans and return them to the pot with 4 quarts fresh cold water.

4  Wrap the herbs and garlic in a 6-inch square of cheesecloth and add it to the pot. Add the carrot, celery, and onion. Bring the water to a low simmer, then cook until the beans are done. Depending on their freshness and the variety of bean, this can take from 45 minutes to 2 hours. Keep checking them for doneness. After 30 minutes of cooking, add the salt.

5  Remove and discard the cheesecloth bundle and the vegetables and drain. Serve the beans warm, drizzled with olive oil.

*(continued)*

1 Pick over the beans to remove any stones or bad or broken beans. Rinse thoroughly.

2 Put the beans in a stockpot and cover with 4 quarts cold water. Bring to a simmer and cook for 2 to 3 minutes. Remove the pot from the heat and let the beans soak in the hot water for 1 hour.

3 Drain the beans and return them to the stockpot. Cover with 4 quarts fresh cold water.

4 Wrap the herbs and garlic in a 6-inch square of cheesecloth and add it to the pot. Add the carrot, celery, and onion. Bring the water to a boil and cook at a low simmer until the beans are done. Depending on their freshness and the variety of bean, this can take from 45 minutes to 2 hours. Keep checking them for doneness. After 30 minutes of cooking, add the salt.

5 Remove and discard the cheesecloth bundle and the vegetables and drain. Serve the beans warm, drizzled with olive oil.

# FAGIOLI ALL' UCCELLETTO

## *Stewed Beans*

While we fancy ourselves bean experts in Tuscany, beans are actually a New World crop that didn't arrive in Italy until the late 1500s, when Columbus sailed back from America. Until then, the only bean that we had in Italy was the black-eyed pea, which came to us by way of Egypt. But we picked up on the idea fast. *Fagioli all'uccelletto* means "beans bird style" and was called that because we cook the beans in the same way that we cook the tiny birds we find in the hills around Tuscany. **SERVES 8, ABOUT 9 CUPS**

¼ cup extra virgin olive oil

6 garlic cloves, crushed

1 tablespoon chopped fresh sage leaves

1 teaspoon crushed red pepper

3 cups canned whole tomatoes, with their juice, pureed or crushed (You can also use pureed or crushed canned tomatoes, but I think the whole ones are less acidic and of higher quality.)

7 cups cooked cannellini beans (see page 187; 3 cups cooking water reserved)

Salt

Freshly ground black pepper

**WINE SUGGESTION:** *This dish is good as an antipasto, too. Serve it with a wine made from Sangiovese grapes—Bolgheri Piastraia or a simple Chianti.*

1  Coat the bottom of a large skillet with the olive oil. Add the garlic and sage and sauté over medium-high heat until the garlic is golden. Add the crushed red pepper and cook 30 seconds.

2  Add the tomatoes and salt and pepper to taste. Cook for 10 minutes.

3  Add the beans, stir, and reduce the heat to medium-low. Cook for 30 minutes, using the reserved bean cooking water (or tap water) as needed to keep the beans moist. Taste for seasonings and serve.

# INSALATA SETTE

## *Seven-Bean Salad*

It's an unwritten law in Italy that you don't mix varieties of beans, whether it's chick-peas, cannellini beans, or any other variety. Don't ask me why—especially since these kinds of combinations are popular even in green salad–loving countries like the United States. I was mulling this over one day while trying to figure out how to use a new 10,000-pound shipment of beans. Then it hit me: Why not make a bean equivalent of the mixed green salad? It's hardly a revolutionary idea for a dish, but it's become for me the one that represents my simple and notch-off-of-tradition approach.

The drawback here is cooking so many types of beans simultaneously. Most people don't have seven burners the way we do in a professional kitchen. I have a couple of solutions: Either split the cooking of the beans over two days, refrigerating the portion you cook first overnight, and then completing the salad the next day. Or, use fewer varieties of beans so you can cook them all at one time. Or, the worst case scenario (in my opinion), use canned beans, rinse them well, and go from there. I don't suggest cooking different types of beans together, though, since every bean will have a different cooking time. **SERVES 6 TO 8**

½ cup each of 7 different dried beans—preferably zolfini, corona, diavolo, cannellini, sorana, borlotti, and angelo (Almost any combination you choose will be fine; you can also use fewer types but then cook more of each. You need 3½ cups total. See Sources on page 221.)

14 garlic cloves

7 sprigs fresh sage

7 sprigs fresh thyme

7 sprigs fresh rosemary

Salt

¾ cup very thinly sliced red onion

1 cup red wine vinegar

¾ cup diced celery

¾ cup chopped fresh Italian parsley

¾ chopped fresh basil leaves

1 cup extra virgin olive oil

1 teaspoon freshly ground black pepper

⅓ teaspoon crushed red pepper

¾ cup seeded and diced ripe tomatoes

---

**WINE SUGGESTION:** *This dish makes a perfect antipasto, so serve it with a white, like Sauvignon Blanc. These days, I'm partial to Con Vento from Castello del Terriccio.*

---

1  Pick over the beans to remove any stones or bad or broken beans. Soak each variety of bean separately overnight in plenty of cold water. (In warm weather, store the soaking beans in the refrigerator; the heat causes them to release too much protein and shortens the salad's shelf life.)

2  Drain the beans and rinse them.. Place each variety in its own pot, with plenty of water. To each pot, add 2 garlic cloves, 1 sprig each of sage, thyme, and rosemary (you can wrap in a 6-inch square of cheesecloth, if you like) and bring to a simmer. Cook the beans until soft (this will vary from 1 to 2 hours, depending on how fresh the beans are). Add salt. Let the beans cool in their cooking water.

3  While the beans are cooling, soak the sliced onions in the vinegar for at least 30 minutes. Drain, discarding vinegar.

4  Remove and discard the garlic and herb sprigs and drain the beans. In a large bowl combine all of the beans with the celery, parsley, basil, red onion, olive oil, black pepper, crushed red pepper, and salt to taste. Toss well, fold in the tomatoes, and serve. (If you refrigerate the salad, before serving, warm it for a minute or two in a skillet to bring out the flavors.)

# TORTINO *di* CARCIOFI
## *Artichoke Soufflé, Tuscan Style*

Artichoke soufflé sounds very fancy, but this is actually a typical home-style dish housewives of a certain era used to make, most likely using aged pecorino or another sheep's milk cheese instead of the Parmesan I suggest. (I like Parmesan because it is sweeter.) Today you are more likely to find this dish in a trattoria during spring artichoke season, when it turns up on hundreds of menus. **SERVES 8**

1 lemon

6 ounces (2 cups) baby artichokes (or the heart and bottom of globe artichoke or frozen hearts)

2 tablespoons extra virgin olive oil

1 tablespoon minced garlic

1 tablespoon finely chopped fresh Italian parsley

1 tablespoon finely chopped fresh marjoram (or oregano)

1 cup dry white wine

Salt

Freshly ground black pepper

9 eggs, separated

¼ cup grated Parmesan cheese, plus a little more for coating the ramekins

2 tablespoons butter, for greasing ramekins

---

**WINE SUGGESTION:** *This soufflé is great as an appetizer, too, and would go well with a white wine made from Trebbiano grapes, like Baracchi.*

---

1 Preheat the oven to 375° F.

2 Fill a bowl with water. Cut the lemon in two and squeeze the juice into the water. Add the squeezed lemon halves to the water, too. If you are using baby artichokes, peel the outer leaves from the artichoke until you reach the part where the leaves are mostly a creamy yellow. Cut the top inch off the artichoke and trim away the stem so that you are left with a golf ball–sized heart. Chop the hearts roughly and place in the lemon water. (For globe artichokes, remove the tough outer leaves and cut the artichokes into wedges. Remove the choke and the soft curly leaves above it. Chop and place in the lemon water.) Set aside. Drain before using.

3  Coat the bottom of a skillet with the olive oil. Add the garlic and sauté it over medium heat until it starts to color. Add the artichokes, herbs and wine.

4  Reduce the wine by half. Add 1½ cups water and season with salt and pepper to taste. Cook until the artichokes are tender and the liquid has evaporated, about 20 to 30 minutes, depending on size. Set aside.

5  In a large bowl vigorously beat together by hand the yolks, the ¼ cup Parmesan, and salt and pepper. Beat 4 to 5 minutes, until the mixture is thick. Set aside.

6  Using an electric mixer, beat the egg whites until they are opaque and very shiny white and form soft peaks. The egg whites should be able to gently hold their shape and should not look dry or grainy.

7  Using a rubber spatula, gently fold one-third of the beaten egg whites into the yolk mixture. Repeat until all of the whites have been incorporated. It is important to do this step very gently, so as not to deflate the egg whites. Gently stir in the reserved artichokes.

8  Butter 8 ramekins or small ovenproof dishes and dust with grated Parmesan. Divide the soufflé base evenly among the ramekins.

9  Transfer the ramekins to a roasting pan. Pour hot water into the roasting pan to come halfway up the sides of the ramekins. Bake for 25 to 30 minutes until the tops are golden brown. Serve immediately in the ramekins.

# INSALATA di LASAGNINO

## Tuscan Coleslaw

I've adopted a lot of American food habits, but one that still gives me trouble is mayonnaise as coleslaw dressing. It's so heavy. I prefer the Italian way, with oil and vinegar, which is more bracing and a better contrast to foods like fried chicken, with which coleslaw is often served. In fact, try this with my Pollo Fritto (page 150) to see if you agree. **SERVES 6 TO 8**

¾ cup thinly sliced red onion

1 cup red wine vinegar

Salt

Freshly ground black pepper

1 pound Savoy cabbage, julienned (5 cups)

1 cup grated carrots

⅓ pound radicchio, julienned

1 tablespoon finely chopped fresh tarragon

1 tablespoon minced jalapeño pepper (seeds removed)

⅓ cup extra virgin olive oil

1 Steep the onion in the red wine vinegar in a small bowl. Sprinkle with salt and pepper and marinate for at least 30 minutes on the counter or up to 24 hours in the refrigerator.

2 Combine the cabbage, carrots, radicchio, tarragon, and jalapeño pepper together in a large bowl. Remove the red onion from the vinegar, reserving it, and add the vinegar to the vegetables.

3 Add 3 tablespoons of the onion vinegar, the olive oil, and salt and pepper to taste and toss well. (Reserve the remaining onion vinegar for another use.) Taste the coleslaw for seasonings. Serve immediately or refrigerate until ready to use.

# BARBAROSSA
## *Roasted Beet Salad*

My mom used to make a salad like this—minus the ginger and horseradish—back when we had a garden years ago. She would boil the beets, which you can do, too, but I like them better roasted. **SERVES 6**

2½ pounds red beets (about 6 of roughly the same size)

2½ pounds golden beets (about 6 of roughly the same size)

6 tablespoons extra virgin olive oil

½ cup red wine vinegar

4 teaspoons grated or finely minced ginger

Salt

Freshly ground black pepper

1 pound Swiss chard, stems cut into 1-inch lengths and leaves chopped (8 cups), or the equivalent amount of well-washed beet tops

1 tablespoon freshly grated horseradish, for serving

1  Preheat the oven to 400° F.

2  Wash and trim the beets, leaving an inch or so of greens to minimize bleeding. Put the beets in a shallow baking dish, pour in ½ cup water, and cover the dish with aluminum foil. Bake until a fork slides in and out of the beets easily. Check the golden beets after 30 minutes; they cook faster than the red, which will take 45 minutes to 1 hour. Remove from the oven and let cool.

3  Keeping the yellow and red beets separate, peel them, and cut into 1-inch cubes. Toss each kind of beet with 2 tablespoons of the olive oil, ¼ cup of the red wine vinegar, 2 teaspoons of the grated ginger, and salt and pepper to taste.

4  Bring a large pot of salted water to a boil. Add the Swiss chard or beet tops and blanch for 3 to 4 minutes. Drain and squeeze out the excess water. Toss with the remaining 2 tablespoons olive oil and sprinkle with salt.

5  Arrange the Swiss chard or beet tops on a serving platter and top with the red and golden beets. Garnish with the grated horseradish and serve.

# DADI *di* ZUCCA

## *Butternut Squash Dice*

I serve this with Oven-Fried Squid (page 26). The cold sweetness of the squash sets off the crunchy calamari perfectly. This would also be good with a pork dish, or fish, or on top of a slice of prosciutto as a *crostino.* **SERVES 6**

1 pound butternut squash

2 tablespoons extra virgin olive oil

¼ teaspoon ground cinnamon

¼ teaspoon grated nutmeg

Salt

Freshly ground black pepper

2 tablespoons capers in brine, rinsed (I prefer capers packed in salt because they have more flavor, but you need to rinse and soak them in water for at least 6 hours before using.)

¼ cup Onion Dressing (recipe follows)

1 Preheat the oven to 400° F.

2 Peel and seed the squash and cut it into ¼-inch dice.

3 Toss the diced squash with the olive oil, sprinkle it with the cinnamon, nutmeg, and salt and pepper to taste, and mix well. Spread the squash on a baking sheet in an even layer and bake for 15 minutes. Stir the squash, return it to the oven, and bake for 15 to 20 minutes, or until cooked through.

4 Transfer the squash to a large bowl, add the capers, onion dressing, and salt and pepper if needed, and toss to combine. Serve immediately or refrigerate until ready for use. If you refrigerate the squash, warm it before serving to bring out the flavors.

# SALSA DI CIPOLLA

*Onion Dressing*

YIELD: 1½ CUPS

2 cups finely chopped red onions

Pinch ground cinnamon

Freshly ground black pepper

3 tablespoons plus ½ cup extra virgin olive oil

1 tablespoon capers in brine, rinsed (I prefer capers packed in salt because they have more flavor, but you need to rinse and soak them in water for at least 6 hours before using.)

Pinch grated nutmeg

Salt

2 teaspoons finely chopped fresh marjoram

¼ cup red wine vinegar

1  Preheat the oven 425° F.

2  In a large bowl toss the chopped red onions with the cinnamon, nutmeg, salt and pepper, and the 3 tablespoons olive oil. Spread in an even layer on a baking sheet and roast in the oven for about 30 minutes, or until golden and crispy. Be sure to stir the onions frequently to prevent burning.

3  Let the onions cool and transfer them to a large bowl. Chop the capers and add them with the marjoram, vinegar, and remaining 1 cup olive oil to the bowl. Combine well and season with salt and pepper to taste.

# POLENTA

## *Basic Polenta*

You can make this up to an hour ahead of time. Keep the polenta warm in a covered *bain marie* over low heat. YIELD 8 CUPS

2½ cups organic cornmeal of any coarseness or quick-cooking cornmeal (see Sources, page 221)

1 tablespoon salt

2½ tablespoons extra virgin olive oil

Pour 2½ quarts cold water into a saucepan. Turn the heat to medium and stir in the cornmeal, salt, and olive oil. When the polenta starts to boil, reduce the heat to a simmer, and cook, stirring constantly, for 40 to 45 minutes. If lumps form, use a whisk to get them out. The polenta is ready when it has the consistency of cream of wheat. If it is too stiff, stir in a little hot water.

# • GUALTIERO MARCHESI •

While many American food lovers know Giuliano Bugialli and Marcella Hazan, it's rare to find someone who has heard of Gualtiero Marchesi, a chef who in the 1980s and 1990s changed the way Italians ate and cooked. Marchesi never promoted himself in the United States, but it's a shame—especially since he had a huge influence on a generation of chefs, myself included, who emigrated to the United States and have been passing on his ideas for years.

When Marchesi first opened his own restaurant in Milan in the 1980s, lots of people were outraged, not only by the prices, but also by his *nouvelle cuisine* ideas, like deconstructed ravioli and adding gold leaf to risotto. Actually the food wasn't revolutionary at all, just well researched—the ravioli was basically made the old-fashioned way and the gold leaf was a fairly common ingredient in medieval times. In truth, people couldn't have minded the prices that much, since the place became an instant destination. Foodies also started to call Marchesi "Il Divino," or The Divine One.

Still, it took a while for aspiring chefs to adjust to the new model. Most stuck to a more traditional route. For me, though, it was all about Marchesi, who was so steeped in both Italian and French traditions and so intellectual in his approach to food. No one else in Italy was cooking like him. For a few months in the late 1980s, I even drove the ten-hour round trip to Milan every Monday just to study with Il Divino. Today, in his seventies, he's still going strong, opening new places like a young Turk. If you've never eaten at one of Marchesi's restaurants, you should make a point of it the next time you're in Rome or Paris or Franciacorta, a small town between Bergamo and Brescia, which has my favorite restaurant of his.

# DOLCI

## *Desserts*

I hate to admit it, but today's pastry chefs don't have anything on the Romans. After the appetizers and main courses had been polished off at a big dinner party, guests would make way for the *secundae mensae*, or second table. The words were literal: Just as guests were finishing the main event, a platoon of slaves would arrive to carry away the dining table. In its place, they'd set up a new one laden with stuffed and fresh fruits, rich honey cakes, pear soufflés, nuts, and lots of wine.

Maybe it dates back to some medieval frugality streak, but Tuscans have never been into sweets the way other Italians are. In fact, when I wrote my first book and had to come up with forty different desserts to fit with the menu format, I was hard-pressed to produce sweet options. At Vipore, my family's restaurant in Lucca, we usually had only two choices for sweets lovers—a rustic fruit tart or *cantucci*, the famous almond biscotti. Anyone who ever ate with us rarely had room for anything else. I'm not personally big on desserts, but the one thing I know is that in the United States, they're your deal-closer. Desserts are what people walk away from a meal thinking about, so you really want them to be special.

I've worked with the most inventive of pastry chefs, who've all been able to channel Tuscany through me. We talk and talk and talk and then they produce some revelation that's both new, yet completely rooted in my tradition. There's not a trattoria in Tuscany that serves chocolate banana upside-down cake—with a big banana chip on top, no less—but at Beppe, it seems both humble and inventive. The same for Meyer lemon *panna cotta* another Beppe dessert. We are very attached to tradition in my corner of the world where *panna cotta* comes in only one flavor: cream. No one even knows what a Meyer lemon is. From my new vantage point in New York, and for anyone who turns up their nose at the idea, all I can say is that's too bad.

# TORTA *di* MIELE

## *Honey Cake*

The Romans didn't use much sugar because it was so expensive. Instead, for cakes like this or anything that needed sweetening, they used honey. There were so many kinds back then, it was actually a seasonal product, with different variations available at different times of the year, and even counterfeit versions of the priciest kinds. Just good old clover honey will work here, but if you want to give this dish a richer flavor, look for chestnut honey. **SERVES 6**

12 tablespoons (1½ sticks) butter at room temperature

1 cup sugar

¾ cup honey

2 eggs

1½ cups flour

1 cup diced dried figs

½ cup chopped walnuts, toasted

---

**WINE SUGGESTION:** *I like a red table wine like Chianti with this, or a Syrah.*

---

1 Preheat the oven to 325° F. Butter and flour a 10- by 3½-inch loaf pan.

2 In a standing electric mixer fitted with the paddle attachment cream together the butter, sugar, and honey.

3 Add the eggs one at a time and continue beating until they are incorporated.

4 Add the flour and mix until it is just combined, stopping occasionally to scrape down the sides of the bowl. Fold in the dried figs and walnuts. Pour the batter into the prepared pan and bake for 40 to 45 minutes, or until a toothpick inserted in the center comes out clean. To unmold, run a knife around the edge of the pan while cake is still hot. Invert onto a cooling rack. You can serve this loaf warm or let it cool. To store any leftover cake, cover with plastic wrap and keep at room temperature.

# TORTA *di* CIOCCOLATO CALDO

## *Molten Chocolate Cake*

Jean-Georges Vongerichten is credited with making this cake with the melting center famous. Even after all these years, when I try to take it off the menu, people complain. The quality of the chocolate is very important here; buy something good, such as Valrhona or El Rey, a Venezuelan chocolate. **SERVES 8**

10 ounces chopped bittersweet chocolate

12 tablespoons (1½ sticks) butter, cut into pieces, plus more for buttering the ramekins

¾ cup confectioner's sugar

¾ cup all purpose flour

1 teaspoon salt

2 tablespoons granulated sugar, for dusting ramekins

3 whole large eggs

3 egg yolks

**WINE SUGGESTION:** *You can just finish off the bottle of red you opened for dinner, or if you want to be fancier, try a Massavecchia, a Tuscan wine made with the Aleatico grape that is very similar to port.*

1  Preheat the oven to 350° F.

2  Melt the chocolate and butter in the top of a double boiler set over simmering water, stirring constantly, until the mixture is smooth and creamy, with a glossy finish. Remove the pan from the heat and let the mixture cool.

3  Combine the confectioner's sugar, flour, and salt.

4  Butter eight 4-ounce ramekins and dust with the granulated sugar.

5  Beat the whole eggs and the egg yolks together with a whisk or an electric mixer until light and thick. Slowly whisk into the cooled chocolate mixture.

6  Fold the dry ingredients into the chocolate mixture until well incorporated. Fill each prepared ramekin three-quarters full with batter. Place on a baking sheet. Bake for 15 minutes. Let cool slightly, then invert each cake on a plate. When cut into with a spoon, molten chocolate should ooze out of the center of the cake.

# TORTA *di* ROSA

## *Rosa's Cake*

This was the only cake my mom made when I was little and I loved it. Now it's one of my daughter's favorites, too. Make the pastry cream in advance or while you're waiting for the cake to cool. **SERVES 10 TO 12**

1 quart plus 1 cup whole milk

½ vanilla bean (or ½ teaspoon vanilla extract)

1¾ cups sugar

6 egg yolks, plus 3 whole eggs

½ cup cornstarch

6 ounces chopped unsweetened chocolate

3 tablespoons extra virgin olive oil

2⅓ cups flour

1 teaspoon grated orange zest

1 teaspoon baking powder

1 teaspoon baking soda

¼ teaspoon vanilla extract

---

**WINE SUGGESTION:** *When my mom made this cake she would just keep drinking the wine she'd had with dinner. I'd go the same route.*

---

1  To make the pastry cream: In a large saucepan, bring 3⅔ cups of the milk, the vanilla bean, and ½ cup of the sugar to a low boil over low heat. Remove the pan from the heat.

2  In the bowl of a standing mixer combine the 6 egg yolks, cornstarch, and ¼ cup of the remaining sugar. Beat on medium speed until pale yellow.

3  With the motor running, slowly pour the hot milk into the yolk mixture, making sure it is well incorporated. Pour the mixture back into the saucepan and return to the heat. Bring to a simmer and cook, stirring constantly, until the pastry cream thickens to the consistency of yogurt. Remove the vanilla bean.

4  Spoon about 2½ cups of the warm pastry cream into a bowl, cover with plastic wrap, and refrigerate until chilled, about 2 hours or up to 24 hours.

5  Add ⅓ cup of the remaining milk to the pastry cream in the saucepan. Add the chocolate and return the pan to the heat, stirring for 3 to 5 minutes, until the chocolate melts and blends with the pastry cream. Spoon the chocolate pastry cream into a bowl, cover with plastic wrap, and refrigerate until chilled, about 2 hours or up to 24 hours.

6  To make the cake: Preheat the oven to 375° F. Grease a 12-inch cake pan.

7  In a large bowl beat the 3 whole eggs with a whisk. Continue whisking as you add in the olive oil, the remaining 1 cup sugar, the flour, the remaining 1 cup milk, orange zest, baking powder, baking soda, and vanilla extract. Using an electric mixer, beat on low speed for 7 minutes. (If you are like my mom, you do this by hand; it takes about 10 minutes.)

8  Pour the batter into the prepared cake pan and bake for 30 minutes, until lightly golden on top and a toothpick inserted into center comes out clean. Let the cake cool completely. Run a knife around the edges of the pan to help release the cake and invert the cake onto a rack. Slice the cake horizontally into three layers.

9  Spread the chocolate pastry cream on top of the bottom layer. Place the middle cake layer on top and spread it with the vanilla pastry cream. Put the remaining cake layer on top and decorate it with any remaining pastry cream. Serve.

# PANNA COTTA *al* LIMONE

## *Meyer Lemon Panna Cotta*

While *flan* and *panna cotta* have similar pudding-like textures, they're made a little differently. Both are cooked on the stove, but *flan* uses eggs as a thickener, while *panna cotta*, or "cooked cream," relies on gelatin. Italians, myself included, are partial to *panna cotta*, but I enjoy mixing things up a little and add Meyer lemon juice, which gives the dessert a nice zing. Serve it with a slice of candied lemon peel on the side. **SERVES** 8

3 sheets gelatin (available in specialty stores)

2 cups heavy cream

1 cup sugar

1 cup minus 2 tablespoons plain whole milk yogurt

1 cup minus 2 tablespoons sour cream

2 tablespoons Meyer lemon juice (if not available, use regular lemon juice) and an extra teaspoon sugar

¾ tablespoon grated Meyer lemon zest

Nonstick cooking spray

---

**WINE SUGGESTION:** *I like Florus Moscadello from Castello Banfi with this. It picks up on the tangy lemon of the dessert.*

---

1 Fill a bowl with cool water. Add the gelatin sheets and let soften.

2 In a medium saucepan bring the heavy cream and sugar to a boil. Remove from the heat. Remove the softened gelatin sheets from the water and add them to the hot cream. Stir to dissolve.

3 Stir in the yogurt, sour cream, Meyer lemon juice, and zest.

4 Coat the inside of eight 6-ounce ramekins with nonstick spray, then fill the ramekins with the lemon mixture. Refrigerate for at least 2 hours or up to 2 days.

5 To serve, unmold each ramekin on a dessert plate and and top with a fresh fruit of choice.

# BOMBOLONCINI

## *Little Doughnuts*

You find recipes for fried dough in many cultures—in Germany, it's krapfen, in Spain, churros—and I know why: Fried dough is deliciously crispy, not too sweet, and best while still warm. The Italian version, *bomboloncini,* are especially popular at the Tuscan seaside, where you can buy them from stands along the road. I'm a purist and like them plain, but lots of my friends like slicing their *bomboloncini* open and spreading them with pastry cream and chocolate sauce or a smear of marmalade. **MAKES ABOUT 50 2-INCH DOUGHNUTS, ENOUGH TO SERVE 5**

1 teaspoon active dry yeast

2½ cups flour

2½ tablespoons sugar, plus more for dusting all the doughnuts

1 teaspoon salt

2½ tablespoons warm milk

2½ tablespoons melted butter

4 egg yolks

1½ quarts vegetable or canola oil, for frying

**WINE SUGGESTION:** *The first time I made these doughnuts, I drank with them the sparkly Piedmont rosé, Brachetto d'Aqui Braeda, made by my friend, Raffaella Bologna. I've yet to find a better combination, so look for something similar.*

1   In a large bowl combine ½ teaspoon of the dry yeast with ½ cup lukewarm water. Let stand for 5 to 10 minutes until the yeast foams, then stir in 2½ cups of the flour. Cover with plastic wrap and put in a warm place for at least 45 minutes, or until the dough has doubled in size.

2   In the bowl of a standing electric mixer, combine the remaining 2½ cups flour, sugar, salt, and the remaining ½ teaspoon yeast. Stir to combine well.

3   Using the paddle attachment on slow speed, beat in the warm milk and melted butter. Add the egg yolks one at a time, beating until the dough is smooth and homogeneous. Cover with plastic wrap and let stand in a warm place for 45 minutes.

*(continued)*

4 Using the electric mixer, combine the two doughs into one. Break off a piece of dough about the size of a softball and roll it out ¼-inch thick on a clean, floured work surface. Cut out doughnut rounds using a 2-inch cookie cutter. Place the rounds on a baking sheet with plenty of room in between, about 15 per sheet. Repeat until all the dough has been cut. Let the rounds rest for at least 15 to 20 minutes, or until they have tripled in size.

5 Pour enough vegetable oil into a deep fryer or stockpot to measure at least 3 inches. Heat to 325° F on a deep-fat thermometer. Fry the doughnuts in batches, about 5 to 10 minutes per batch, until they are golden brown and very puffy. Drain on paper towels and keep in a warm place until all doughnuts are cooked. Toss the doughnuts in sugar while still warm and serve.

# FAGIOLI FRITTI

## *Bean Fritters*

About a year after I opened Beppe, I launched a business called the Republic of Beans to import dried beans from Italy. I stocked up on 10,000 pounds, which pretty much took up all of our office space. Beans spilled out everywhere, even from the filing cabinets. And while my bean dishes were selling well, I needed to use up the beans fast so we could at least get to our desks. When I was invited in January 2002 to cook at the James Beard House, I got a brainstorm and chose beans as the evening's theme. From start to finish, I shoehorned beans into as many dishes as I could, including this dessert I invented—a variation on the doughnut. **MAKES ABOUT 80 FRITTERS, TO SERVE 6**

3 cups cooked white beans (see page 187)

3 eggs

2 tablespoons extra virgin olive oil

1 tablespoon rum

3 tablespoons granulated sugar

7 tablespoons plus 1 teaspoon flour

1½ teaspoons baking soda

Pinch salt

Pinch freshly ground black pepper

6 cups canola or peanut oil, for frying

Confectioner's sugar, for sprinkling

**WINE SUGGESTION:** *I like these fritters with a young Vin Santo.*

1  Puree the cooked beans in a food processor until smooth. Transfer to a large bowl.

2  Stir in the eggs, olive oil, rum, granulated sugar, flour, baking soda, and salt and pepper, and combine well. The batter should be firm, but still slightly runny.

3  Pour enough canola oil into a deep fryer or stockpot to measure at least 3 inches. Heat to 350° F. on a deep-fat thermometer. Drop the batter by the tablespoon into the hot oil and fry in batches until golden brown, about 4 minutes. Drain the fritters on paper towels and keep in a warm place until all the fritters are made. Sprinkle the fritters with confectioner's sugar and serve.

# GELATO *di* MASCARPONE

## *Mascarpone Ice Cream*

I'd always heard that Catherine de' Medici brought the first ice cream with her to France, but sadly, this seems to be a bit of historical misinformation. Experts say that the Chinese actually invented ice cream, and it didn't arrive until the early 1500s in Italy, where people thought it was a chemist's party trick of some sort. It wasn't used for food until the Neapolitans and Florentines started eating sorbet in the 1660s. Mascarpone, a rich cheese from Lombardy, makes this like a double-cream vanilla. You need an ice cream maker to make this recipe. **YIELD: 1 QUART**

5 egg yolks

½ cup sugar

3 tablespoons light corn syrup

2 cups whole milk

½ cup heavy cream

½ cup mascarpone

**WINE SUGGESTION:** *I would go with* limoncello, *Italy's lemony liqueur. You can even drizzle some on top of the ice cream, if you like.*

1 Fill a large bowl with water and ice cubes and set the ice bath aside.

2 In another large bowl combine the egg yolks, ¼ cup of the sugar, and the corn syrup and whisk until smooth.

3 In a medium saucepan combine the milk, heavy cream, and remaining ¼ cup sugar and scald over low heat. Pour one-third of the hot milk mixture into the egg yolk/sugar mixture and whisk until combined, about 10 seconds. Immediately pour the mixture back into the pan with the milk mixture, whisking constantly. Bring the mixture back to just under a boil over medium-low heat. Remove the pan from the heat and stir in the mascarpone. Transfer to a bowl.

4 Cool the ice cream mixture to 40 degrees by setting it in the ice bath.

5 Strain the mixture into the bowl of an ice cream maker. Churn for 10 to 15 minutes, or according to the manufacturer's directions. (Or fill a large bowl with ice and nestle the bowl with the ice cream mixture on top. Stir constantly for 20 minutes, or until thick.) Serve immediately or freeze. Use within 2 days, "warming" in the refrigerator for 30 minutes before serving.

# BISCOTTI di SESAMO
## Sesame Cookies

Ancient Indians thought sesame seeds were the key to immortality. The Chinese used sesame oil to light their lamps. In Italy, we just liked the way sesame tasted and started importing the seeds during Roman times from Egypt and Persia. Today sesame seeds are more common in southern Italy than northern, but you can still find them in cookies like these in Tuscan bakeries. Make sure to use fresh sesame seeds; they can go bad quickly.

MAKES ABOUT 100 COOKIES

16 tablespoons (2 sticks) butter, softened

2 cups light brown sugar

2 eggs

3 cups flour

1 teaspoon baking powder

½ teaspoon baking soda

½ teaspoon salt

1¾ cups sesame seeds, toasted

WINE SUGGESTION: *Vin Santo is the way to go here. It's perfect for dipping these biscotti.*

1  Preheat the oven to 375° F.

2  In a standing electric mixer fitted with the paddle attachment cream the butter and brown sugar.

3  Add the eggs, one at a time, beating well after each addition.

4  Gradually add the flour, baking powder, baking soda, salt, and half of the sesame seeds. Mix until just combined, occasionally scraping down the sides of the bowl.

5  Roll the dough into 1-inch balls. Roll the balls in the remaining sesame seeds. Flatten the balls into ¼-inch disks and place on greased cookie sheets, spaced one inch apart. Bake for 10 minutes. Transfer the cookies to racks to cool. They will keep in an airtight container for 1 to 2 weeks.

# CENCI FRITTI

## *Fried Ribbons*

If you've ever been to Carnevale (Italian Mardi Gras) in Viareggio, you've almost certainly had *cenci*. Restaurants serve piles of them dusted with confectioner's sugar, and back when families celebrated Carnevale at home, making *cenci* was an all-inclusive activity, with even toddlers pitching in. **MAKES 40 TO 45 COOKIES**

4 cups all-purpose flour

¾ cup sugar

1 tablespoon grated lemon zest

Pinch salt

1 teaspoon baking soda

1 teaspoon baking powder

8 tablespoons (1 stick) butter, cut into pea-sized pieces

4 eggs

¼ cup Vin Santo

Vegetable or peanut oil, for frying

Granulated sugar, for dusting

Confectioner's sugar, for dusting

**WINE SUGGESTION:** *Asti Spumante is my choice to go with these cookies.*

1　In a large bowl combine the flour, sugar, lemon zest, salt, baking powder, and baking soda.

2　Add the butter to the flour mixture. Working quickly, using your fingers, rub the butter into the flour until well combined.

3　Make a well in the flour/butter mixture and add the eggs and Vin Santo. Using your hands, start to combine the mixture into a dough. Knead for a few minutes, then cover the dough with plastic wrap and place in the refrigerator for at least 30 minutes or up to 48 hours.

4　Roll out the dough ¼ inch thick on a floured surface. Cut the dough into rectangles 1½ by 4 inches. In the center of each rectangle make 2 lengthwise scores, without cutting all the way through the dough.

5　Pour enough oil into a large skillet to measure 4 inches deep. Heat to 350° F. on a deep-fat thermometer.

6　Twist each dough rectangle one or two times and place immediately in the hot oil. Fry in batches about 3 to 4 minutes on each side, until golden brown. Transfer the fried dough to paper towels to drain. Dust the cookies with granulated sugar and confectioner's sugar and serve immediately.

# BISCOTTI *di* CIOCCOLATO
## *Chocolate Cookies*

You won't find these cookies in any Tuscan bakery because my pastry chef at Beppe invented them. I'm sure they'd be a hit even in Lucca, since I get more requests for this recipe than almost anything else on the menu. **MAKES 100 COOKIES**

1½ cups (3 sticks) butter, softened

1¾ cups sugar

1 tablespoon rum

2 eggs

3 cups all-purpose flour

1¾ cups (6 ounces) unsweetened cocoa powder

1 teaspoon baking powder

**WINE SUGGESTION:** *A Tuscan red made from Merlot, Cabernet, or Aleatico grapes would be great.*

1  Preheat the oven to 325° F. Grease two cookie sheets.

2  In a standing electric mixer fitted with the paddle attachment cream together the butter, sugar, and rum.

3  Add the eggs, one at a time.

4  When the eggs are thoroughly combined, gradually add the flour, cocoa powder, and baking powder, stopping occasionally to scrape down the sides of the bowl. Mix until the ingredients are just combined.

5  Roll the dough into 1-inch balls. Place about ¾ inch apart on two prepared cookie sheets and bake for 5 minutes. Cool on racks. The cookies will keep in an airtight container for 1 to 2 weeks.

# BRUTTI MA BUONI

## Ugly but Tasty

The recipe for these meringues was imported to Tuscany from Piedmont when Florence briefly reigned as Italy's capital. In Prato, they're considered the sister sweet to the famous *cantucci*. I love their light crunchiness. MAKES 100 COOKIES

5 cups blanched almonds

1½ cups sugar

¼ teaspoon ground cinnamon

½ cup candied fruit, finely chopped (optional)

Salt

7 egg whites

WINE SUGGESTION: *Pack a box of these cookies and a bottle of Chardonnay for a perfect picnic ending.*

1 Preheat the oven to 325° F. Grease two cookie sheets.

2 Place the almonds on a baking sheet and toast until lightly colored, 8 to 10 minutes.

3 In a food processor coarsely chop 2½ cups of the toasted almonds and transfer them to a bowl. Finely grind the remaining almonds, then add them to the coarsely chopped almonds, along with the sugar, cinnamon, and candied fruit if using. Set aside.

4 Add a pinch of salt to the egg whites and using an electric mixer on the second highest speed beat to medium peaks. Fold a third of the egg whites at a time into the almond mixture.

5 Drop the batter in tablespoon scoops about 1½ inches apart onto the prepared cookie sheets. Bake until the cookies are golden brown, 15 to 20 minutes. Cool on racks. The cookies will keep in an airtight container for 1 to 2 weeks.

# MANGIA *e* BEVI
## *Eat and Drink*

This is a wonderful summertime dessert that was popular in Italy in the 1980s. When my dad would take me to a nearby *gelateria* as a treat, it was the first thing I ordered. I liked the little paper flags the shop used as a garnish as much as the fruit and ice cream. **SERVES** 8

1½ teaspoons grated lemon zest

½ cup Gran Gala or other orange liqueur

⅓ cup orange juice

½ cup dry white wine

3 cups diced peaches

1½ cups diced fresh apricots

1½ cups grapes

1 cup diced plums

2 cups diced cantaloupe

1 cup quartered strawberries

1 cup blueberries

1 cup blackberries

1 cup raspberries

3 cups seeded diced watermelon

1 tablespoon chopped mint leaves

½ cup sugar

1 pint vanilla ice cream (or sorbet of your choice), softened

1 cup heavy cream

½ cup Cherry Compote (page 217)

Miniature flags or umbrellas, for decoration

---

**WINE SUGGESTION:** *Whichever liqueur is left over after making the recipe.*

---

1  Combine the lemon zest, Gran Gala, orange juice, and wine in a large saucepan and heat over medium heat until the mixture starts to simmer. Cook for 5 minutes. Remove the pan from the heat and cool the marinade for 10 minutes.

2  Mix all of the fruit together in a large bowl. Pour the marinade over the fruit and mix well. Cover the bowl with plastic wrap and refrigerate for 2 hours or up to 24 hours.

3  To assemble, you need 8 large glasses. Spoon in layers into each glass: 4 tablespoons fruit; 4 tablespoons ice cream; 2 tablespoons fruit; 2 tablespoons heavy cream; 1 tablespoon fruit; 1 tablespoon cherry compote. Top with a miniature flag or umbrella and serve.

# INSALATA *di* COCOMERO

## *Watermelon Salad*

I recently found an old recipe for watermelon that called for chunks of the fruit tossed with anise seed. Inspired, I substituted Sambuca, an anise-flavored liqueur that we love in Italy. Sambuca is also good poured over melon sorbet. **SERVES 4 TO 6**

2 teaspoons grated orange zest

2 star anise

¾ cup Sambuca

¼ cup sugar (optional)

9 cups cubed seeded watermelon

**WINE SUGGESTION**: *Honestly, this dessert has enough of a kick on its own!*

1 Combine the orange zest, ½ cup water, anise stars, Sambuca, and sugar if using in a saucepan, bring to a simmer, and cook for 5 minutes.

2 Remove the pan from the heat and strain the syrup into a large bowl. Let cool for 15 minutes, then stir in the watermelon. Marinate for 2 hours or up to 24 hours. Serve. Leftovers will keep in a covered container in the refrigerator for a few days.

# COMPOSTA *di* CILIEGIE
## *Cherry Compote*

I started making compote in the United States because it was so hard to find the Italian cherry sauce, *amarena fabbri*, here. I like this dessert even better than that sauce. I spoon it over really good vanilla ice cream or a great cake, like Rosa's Cake (page 204). I also use this same approach to make all kinds of berry compotes. **ABOUT 2 CUPS, SERVING 2 TO 4**

½ cup sugar

4 cups pitted Bing cherries or sour cherries

1 In a large saucepan stir together the sugar, ½ cup water, and the cherries, bring to a low boil, and cook for 15 to 20 minutes, when the cherries start to soften.

2 Remove the pan from the heat and let cool. Serve. Any leftover compote will keep in a covered container in the refrigerator for a few days.

# INSALATA di PESCHE

## Peach Salad

This is a popular dish in summer when peaches are at their peak. Really old recipes call for poaching the fruit in the sauce, but I like marinating the fruit better; it tastes fresher to me.

SERVES 3 TO 4

3 cups white wine, red wine, or Champagne

¼ cup orange juice

⅓ cup sugar

1½ tablespoons lemon juice

2 lemon verbena leaves or mint sprigs

4½ cups thinly sliced peaches

WINE SUGGESTION: *The wine you used in making the salad.*

1 Combine the wine, orange juice, sugar, lemon juice, and lemon verbena or mint in a saucepan, bring to a simmer, and cook for 20 minutes. Remove the pan from the heat.

2 Put the peaches in a large bowl. Pour the marinade over them and mix well. Place the bowl in the refrigerator and marinate for at least 3 hours but no longer than 24 hours. Any leftover peach salad will keep in a covered container in the refrigerator for a few days.

# MISTO *di* BOSCO

## *Fruit of the Woods*

I used to serve this at Vipore, my family's restaurant in Lucca, as soon as berries came in season. You can obviously change the kind of berries and the proportions, too. I like adding a spoonful to a glass of Prosecco. **SERVES 4**

2 cups currants

2 cups blackberries

2 cups raspberries

3 tablespoons sugar

2 tablespoons Gran Gala or other fruit liqueur

---

**WINE SUGGESTION:** *Spumante or any other light sparkling wine.*

---

Place all of the ingredients in a large bowl and toss well. Cover with plastic wrap and refrigerate for 2 hours before serving. Any leftovers will keep in a covered container in the refrigerator for a few days.

# SOURCES

✤

**Adriana's Caravan**
Grand Central Market
43rd Street and Lexington Avenue
New York, NY 10016
800-316-0820
www.adrianascaravan.com
A large selection of gourmet specialties. Great source for spices.

**A.G. Ferrari Foods**
14324 Catalina Street
San Leandro, CA 94577
877-878-2783
www.agferrari.com
Imported Italian food products, ranging from artisan olive oils and balsamic vinegars to rustic pastas like fregola and sauces.

**Buon Italia**
75 Ninth Avenue
New York, NY 10011
212-633-9090
www.buonitalia.com
Retail shop and wholesaler, featuring food products imported from Italy, including fregola, located in New York's Chelsea Market.

**Dean and Deluca**
560 Broadway
New York, NY 10013
or
697 South St. Helena Highway
St. Helena, CA 94574
800-221-7714
www.dean-deluca.com
Cured meats, cheeses, olive oil, vinegar, cookware, and specialty produce.

**Kalustyan's**
123 Lexington Avenue
New York, NY 10016
212-685-3451
Kalustyans.com
Retail shop with wholesale and mail-order available, featuring an extensive selection of spices and herbs.

**Murray's Cheese Shop**
257 Bleecker Street
New York, NY 10014
www.Murrayscheese.com
Extensive cheese selection, olives, oils, pasta, vinegar, and imported specialty items.

**Peck**
Via Victor Hugo 4
Milan, 20123 Italy
+39 02876774
www.peck.it
Since 1883, Peck has styled itself "the Temple of Italian Gastronomy"; for the Milanese, this favorite luxury delicatessen is on a par with Fauchon in Paris or Harrods in London.

**Republic of Beans**
212-579-3248
www.republicofbeans.com
info@republicofbeans.com.
Chef Cesare Casella's imported selection of oils and spices, including Tuscan Spice, and this year's crop of specialty heirloom Italian beans. The company also stocks fennel pollen and Italian sea salts.

**The Sausage Maker**
1500 Clinton Street, Bldg 123
Buffalo, NY 14206-3099
888-490-8525
www.sausagemaker.com
A well-stocked home sausage-making equipment supply and manufacturing company.

**Sur La Table**
Seattle Design Center
5701 Sixth Avenue South, Suite 486
Seattle, WA 98108
800-243-0852 or 866-328-5412
www.surlatable.com
A reliable source of top-quality cookware and hard-to-find kitchen tools, including the terra-cotta chicken press.

**Williams-Sonoma**
3250 Van Ness Avenue
San Francisco, CA 94109
877-812-6235
www.Williams-sonoma.com
One of the first American retailers to make professional cooking equipment and gourmet foods widely available to home cooks.

**Wegmans Food Markets**
800-WEGMANS
www.wegmans.com
1500 Brook Avenue
P.O. Box 30844
Rochester, NY 14603-0844
This East Coast chain of grocery stores carries a broad selection of Italian products, including hard-to-find cheeses, beans, and extra virgin olive oils.

**Zabar's**
2245 Broadway
New York, NY 10024
800-697-6301
www.Zabars.com
Cheese, cured meats, fish, produce, cookware, and specialty items.

# BIBLIOGRAPHY

Apicius. *Cooking and Dining in Imperial Rome*. Edited and translated by Joseph Dommers Vehling. New York: Dover Publications, Inc., 1977.

Editors of *Cooks Illustrated*. *Baking Illustrated: The Practical Kitchen Companion for the Home Baker With 350 Recipes You Can Trust*. Brookline, MA: America's Test Kitchen, 2004.

Bugialli, Giuliano. *Bugialli on Pasta*. New York: Stewart, Tabori & Chang, 2000.

Dalby, Andrew, and Grainger, Sally. *The Classical Cookbook*. Los Angeles: J. Paul Getty Museum, 1996.

Edwards, John. *The Roman Cookery of Apicius*. Washington: Hartley & Marks, 1984.

Grant, Mark. *Roman Cookery: Ancient Recipes for Modern Kitchens*. London: Serif, 1999.

Hazan, Marcella. *The Classic Italian Cookbook*. New York: Ballantine Books, 1973.

Lami, Miti Vigliero. *L'Alice delle Meraviglie*. Venice: Marsilio Editori, 1998.

Machlin, Edda Servi. *The Classic Cuisine of the Italian Jews*. Croton-on-Hudson, NY: Giro Press, 1981.

Parenti, Giovanni Righi. *La Cucina Toscana*. Rome: Newton & Compton Editori, 1995.

———. *La Grande Cucina Toscana*. Milan: SugarCo Edizioni Srl, 1976.

Pradelli, Alessandro Molinari. *La Toscana Com'era*. Rome: Newton & Compton Editori, 1986.

Rinaldi, Mariangela, and Vicini Mariangela. *Buon Appetito, Your Holiness*. New York: Arcade, 1998.

Root, Waverley. *The Food of Italy*. New York: Vintage, 1971.

Santini, Aldo. *La Cucina Fiorentina*. Padova: Franco Muzio Editore, 1992.

Simenti, Mary Taylor. *Pomp and Sustenance: Twenty-five Centuries of Sicilian Food*. Hopewell, N. J.: The Ecco Press, 1998.

Vesco, Clotilde. *Cucina Etrusca: 2685 Anni Dopo*. Florence: Vallecchi Editore, 1985.

Wright, Clifford A. *A Mediterranean Feast*. New York: William Morrow and Company, Inc., 1999.

# INDEX